# PRAYERS FOR A LIFETIME

*Karl Rahner*

# PRAYERS
# FOR A
# LIFETIME

*Edited by*
**Albert Raffelt**

*With an Introduction by*
**Karl Lehmann**

Crossroad • New York

1986

The Crossroad Publishing Company
370 Lexington Avenue, New York, N.Y. 10017

Originally published as *Gebete des Lebens*
© Verlag Herder Freiburg im Breisgau 1984

Translation of the Introduction, the Afterword, and
the prayers In Praise of Creation, Following Christ
Through Love of Neighbor, God's Word as Personal Promise,
Meeting Jesus, Freed by God, Prayer for the Church, Prayer
of a Lay Person, Prayer for Justice and Brotherhood,
Prayer for Peace, The Resurrection of the Dead, and Prayer
for the Reunion of All Christians are copyright ©
1984 by The Crossroad Publishing Company.
See also pages 171-172 which constitute an extension of this copyright page.

Printed in the United States of America

*Library of Congress Cataloging in Publication Data*

Rahner, Karl, 1904–1984
Prayers for a lifetime.

Translation of: Gebete des Lebens.
1. Prayers.    I. Raffelt, Albert.    II. Title.
BV245.R2813    1984        242'.802        84-17585
ISBN 0-8245-0678-2
ISBN 0-8245-0730-4 (pbk.)

# CONTENTS

v

Contents · vii

# INTRODUCTION

An important topic in the theology of our time is the dichotomy that exists between its academic endeavors and the spirituality of the Christian faith. In his essay "Theology and Holiness" (1948), which is still well known today and with good reason, Hans Urs von Balthasar sees this separation in the making ever since the High Middle Ages, and he pleads for a new unity. Traditional dogmatics appeared to be all bone without flesh; spiritual-ascetical literature seemed to many all flesh without bone. However, attempts have been repeatedly made in various quarters to overcome this division. One has only to think of the programs that were drafted in the 1930s and 1940s for a "kneeling," a "praying," and a kerygmatic theology (theology of proclamation).

In the interim, new developments have come to the fore, lending a different shape to systematic theology. The influences, for example, of personalist and existentialist philosophies as well as the biblical salvation-history approach have

lifted the division between thinking and being, between theoretical reason and practical reason. Of course, a number of
other causes continue to play a role in helping to overcome the
estrangement of thought from life: the liturgical movement,
the renewal based on the sources of Holy Scripture and the
Church Fathers, and the return to the original conceptions of
the great saints and the founders of religious orders.

Karl Rahner, together with other theologians, ranks among
the pioneers who remained dissatisfied with the unfamiliarity
with life of traditional theology. Despite their proximity in
Innsbruck, Karl Rahner did not join the efforts of his fellow
Jesuits on behalf of the theology of proclamation. Owing to his
gifts as a philosopher, he could not accept the charge of bank-
ruptcy leveled against the intellectual power of believing
reason. The spirituality of Saint Ignatius Loyola (authentically
imparted to him by his brother Hugo) and, simultaneously, the
study of patristic theology opened up new paths for him. The
anthologies *Rechenschaft des Glaubens* and *The Practice of
Faith* (see the Afterword) provide ample evidence of this new
point of view, which can also be demonstrated of E. Krebs,
K. Adam, G. Söhngen, E. Przywara, H. U. von Balthasar, H. de
Lubac, and Y. Congar.

Sensitive areas in the relationship between theology and
spirituality include instruction on praying and the practice of
prayer. The great theologians were frequently great teachers of
prayer as well. The names of Augustine, Thomas Aquinas, and
Bonaventure prove this, as does a glance at Martin Luther, Karl
Barth, and Dietrich Bonhoeffer. Therefore it seemed useful to
view Rahner's work in this way. The most important of his
statements on the theology of prayer are available in the two
anthologies already mentioned (see the Afterword for refer-
ences). This third anthology devoted to Rahner's thought was
thus able to concentrate on examples of prayer itself.

Even in his early years it was clear that for Rahner prayer
was hardly a secondary topic. "Why We Need to Pray" was the
title of his first essay, written over sixty years ago while he was
in his twenties. Alongside the exacting philosophical works
*Spirit in the World* and *Hearers of the Word* stand the prayers,
arising from a profoundly religious experience, of *Encounters*

*with Silence,* his first book in fact. In 1949, writing under the pseudonym A. Trescher (his mother's maiden name), Rahner published a series of highly personal meditations entitled *Heilige Stunde und Passionsandacht* (appearing in English as *Watch and Pray with Me*). His reserve in publishing such deeply personal and revealing prayers is quite understandable. However, again and again, individual items saw publication. Frequently the *Spiritual Exercises* of Saint Ignatius served as inspiration, as in the case of *Prayers for Meditation* (written with Hugo Rahner), *Spiritual Exercises,* and *Servants of the Lord,* in addition to student days of recollection, Advent sermons, radio talks, and meditations delivered to various groups. During the 1970s, Rahner's prayers, which had been scattered about and difficult to locate, began to appear again.

Karl Rahner possessed a broad understanding of prayer. Every significant experience—whether of joy or of anguish—points the way to the land of unbounded hope wherein God dwells. To the question "Do you pray?" Rahner once replied: "I hope that I pray. You see, whenever I actually notice, in all the big and little moments of my life, how close I am to that unutterable, holy, and loving mystery that we call God, and whenever I place myself there, dealing with this mystery, as it were, in confidence, hope, and love, whenever I accept this mystery, then I pray—and I hope that I do." Prayer is thus a manifold witness to faith expressing itself through speech.

The reader will find in this anthology many prayers that grew out of certain definite situations and reveal characteristic expressions: the prayer of an ordinand on the eve of ordination, collective prayer during Benediction of the Blessed Sacrament, prayer in a sermon on Mary during May devotions, at Christmas, and so on. With great deliberation, Rahner derives the utmost from the seven last words of Jesus on the cross. He also recognizes the abiding significance of fixed formulas of prayer. So, for example, in a letter written in 1982 to a young person, he gives the following advice: "As crazy as it may sound today, I would strongly recommend that you try reciting the rosary just once by yourself alone. Provided that one does not become impatient and that one tries to adjust to the practice slowly,

the quiet, automatic repetition of the words and a consideration of the mysteries of the life of Jesus recalled in the rosary
can summon forth that true stillness in which one dwells
before God." There are also litanies as well as very brief prayers
that are almost ejaculations. With Rahner's understanding of
prayer, it is scarcely a question of mere literary style. On this
score, the present volume contains numerous examples of
prayer from all phases of Rahner's life that more than anything
resemble highly personal meditations and reflections. At this
point, the nuances fade away. The newest, previously unpublished prayers in this book* show above all else that sometimes a stage can be reached in which deep personal concern
and a heightened reflective character become predominant.

It is therefore no surprise that Rahner's religious idiom
changed over the course of almost fifty years. One can easily
see, for example, how the transformation in his christological
thinking is reflected in the various prayers addressed to Jesus.
The reader can also detect glaring contrasts in Rahner's experience of the Church by comparing the early prayer "God of Law"
with the much more recent, almost angry "Prayer for the
Church." In this way, the prayers of Karl Rahner clarify his
path as a Christian, a Jesuit, and a theologian. This many-
layered aspect of these prayers should not be ignored. There is
always a cry from the depths, sometimes faint and restrained,
but always provocative and straightforward. Prayers such as
these exact a high price: quite often the language is that of a
wounded spirit. Anyone who publishes prayers and doesn't
bother to touch them up with literary polish is vulnerable to
attack.

This collection of prayers will reveal to the reader the heart
of Karl Rahner's spirituality, but it can also disclose the intimate relationship between piety and theology in his thought.

---

Namely: In Praise of Creation, Prayer for the Church, Prayer of a Lay Person,
Prayer for Justice and Brotherhood, Prayer for Peace, Prayer to Saint Thomas
Aquinas, The Resurrection of the Dead, and Prayer for the Reunion of All
Christians.

The virtually endless literature on Rahner has, with few exceptions, taken little notice of this. Yet without this added dimension, the distinctive character of Rahner's theology would be severely misjudged. "For in the end all abstract theology winds up in a vacuum if it cannot rise from mere words about a particular topic to prayer, wherein that which has previously only been spoken about may yet happen." It is in this spirit above all that *Prayers for a Lifetime* should serve as a guide to prayer.

## Note to the Third Impression

Karl Rahner's readers and friends have received this book with particular joy and unusual interest. When one thinks of his words immediately above on the incomparable importance of prayer, it is perhaps more than a coincidence that this work was the last book to appear during his lifetime and so should be seen as his parting admonition, his testament to us. It is a fitting completion to the work that in this third impression a prayer could be added that was composed during the final weeks of his life (see the Afterword for details).

*May 1984*
                                                     *Karl Lehmann*
                                                     *Bishop of Mainz*

# BEFORE GOD

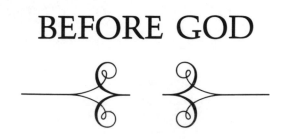

# OPENING

It is both terrible and comforting to dwell in the inconceivable nearness of God, and so to be loved by God Himself that the first and last gift is infinity and inconceivability itself. But we have no choice. God is with us.

## BEFORE GOD

Almighty, Holy God, to You I come, to You I pray. I acknowledge You, Father, Son and Holy Spirit, praise You, glorify You and adore You. I give You thanks for Your great glory.

What can I say to You, my God? Shall I collect together all the words which praise Your holy Name, shall I give You all the names of this world, You, the Unnameable? Shall I call You God of my life, meaning of my existence, hallowing of my acts, my journey's end, bitterness of my bitter hours, home of my loneliness, You my most treasured happiness? Shall I say: Creator, Sustainer, Pardoner, Near One, Distant One, Incomprehensible One, God both of flowers and stars, God of the gentle wind and of terrible battles, Wisdom, Power, Loyalty, and Truthfulness, Eternity and Infinity, You the All-merciful, You the Just One, You Love itself?

What can I say to You, my God? Shall I reproach You with being so far from me or with Your silence which is so terrible and lasts a life-time? Shall I complain because I cannot understand Your forbearance and because Your ways, O Lord, which we, not You, must tread, are so incomprehensibly, hidden and incalculable? But how can I reproach You with Your distance, when I find Your nearness equally mysterious; with Your forbearance, when I owe my sinful life to it; with the incomprehensibility of Your ways, when it is the wickedness and confusion of my own will which has complicated them?

What can I say to You, my God? Should I consecrate myself to You? Should I say that I belong to You with all that I have and am? O my God, how can I give myself to You, unless Your grace accepts me? How can I devote myself to Your service, unless You call me? I give You thanks for having called me. Though I find it so hard to serve You, my weak and cowardly heart must learn to be silent and not to complain. Rather should my mouth belie my heart—which wants to remonstrate with You— because in doing so it tells me of Your truth, which is more important than mine: Indeed, Lord, Your service is good, Your yoke is sweet and Your burden light. I thank You for all that You have asked of me in my life. Be praised for the time in which I was born, glorified for my hours of happiness and my days of misery, blessed for everything that You have denied me. Lord, though I am a lazy and headstrong servant, never dismiss me from Your service. You have power over my heart. You have power over me even in the depths of my soul, where I alone am master of my eternal fate, for Your grace is the grace of eternal omnipotence. Wise, merciful, loving God, do not cast me from Your presence. Keep me in Your service all the days of my life. Ask of me what You will. Only grant what You command of me. Even if I tire in Your service, You in Your patience will not tire of me. You will come to help, You will give me the strength to make a fresh start again and again; to hope against hope; in all my defeats to have faith in victory and in Your triumph within me.

What can I say to You, my God, but that I am a sinner? But You know that better than I and I would certainly neither believe nor admit it, if Your word did not testify against me. Lord, do not depart from me, for I am a sinful man. Surely it is better to make this my appeal? Where, if not with You, could I take refuge in my weakness, in my spiritual sloth, in the duplicity and unreliability even of what is best in me? God of sinners, God of the habitual, daily, cowardly sinner, of the ordinary sinner! O God, there is nothing grand about my sin; it is so everyday, so normal, so much the accepted thing, that I can easily overlook it—only of course, when I overlook You, Most

Holy One, and when I forget that You love us with a jealous love and want to possess our hearts, whole and undivided, burning and ready for anything. O God, whither could I flee? The great sinners could perhaps sate themselves for a time with the diabolical enormity of their sins. But what disgust I feel for my wretchedness, my complacent slowness of heart, the frightening mediocrity of my "good conscience." Only You could continue to tolerate such a heart, only You could continue to love me so patiently. You alone are greater than my poor heart (1 John 3:20). God of sinners, God even of the lukewarm and the slow of heart, have mercy on me!

Behold, O God, I enter Your presence: God, holy and just, You who are Truth, Loyalty, Serenity, Justice, Goodness. In Your presence I must needs prostrate myself as Moses did and say with Peter: Depart from me for I am a sinful man (Luke 5:8). I know that there is only one thing that I can say to You: Have mercy on me. I need Your mercy, because I am a sinner. I am unworthy of Your mercy, because I am a sinner. But I humbly desire Your unfailing mercy, for I am a being of this world, not yet lost; one who still longs for the heavens of Your goodness, who willingly and with tears of joy receives the inexhaustible gift of Your mercy.

Lord, look upon me, see my misery. To whom should I flee, if not to You? How could I tolerate myself, but for the thought that You can tolerate me, but for the knowledge that You are still my friend? Look upon my misery. Look upon Your servant who is lazy, headstrong and superficial. Look upon the meanness of my heart, which offers You only as much as is absolutely necessary and will not be generous in loving You. Look upon my prayers: see how sullenly and reluctantly I fulfill this duty and how cheerfully, for the most part, my heart turns from talking with You to other things. Look upon my work: it is barely satisfactory, extorted from me by the pressure of daily life, rarely prompted by true love of You. Listen to my words: the words of selfless kindness and love are rare. Look upon me, O God: You will see no great sinner, only a small one; one whose very sins are small, mean and commonplace; whose will and heart, mind and strength are mediocre in every respect, even in wickedness. But, my God, when I really reflect on this, I am greatly afraid. Surely the things I am forced to say of myself are precisely those which characterize the lukewarm heart? And have You not said that You prefer a cold heart to a lukewarm one (Apoc 3:16)? Is not my mediocrity the cloak behind which I hide the worst thing of all, in the hope that it will not be discovered: a selfish and cowardly heart, a dull and insensitive heart which knows no generosity of spirit nor breadth of mind?

Have pity on my poor heart, magnanimous and loving God, God of blessed abundance. Send Your Holy Spirit into my poor barren heart and refashion it. May Your Spirit burn deep into my dead heart with the fear of Your judgment and let my heart awaken! May Your Holy Spirit fill it with fear and trembling: let it shake off the deathly grip of hopelessness and resignation! May Your Spirit make my heart humble and contrite: let it be filled with longing for Your sanctity and with confidence in Your all-powerful grace! May Your Spirit fill my heart with the holy penitence which is the beginning of the heavenly life and with confidence in the invincible power of Your assistance, which brings courage and readiness, cheerfulness and boldness to the hearts which serve You.

Only if You give me Your grace, can I feel how much I need it. Only the gift of Your mercy makes me recognize and confess that I am a poor sinner. Only Your love gives me the courage to hate myself without despairing.

You have had mercy on me, Holy God. Your Son has given His Body for me. This is why I can call upon Your mercy. He has tasted death, which is the wages of sin (Rom 6:23). This is why I need not despair in the sinful darkness of my life. I venerate the mystery which shows the death of the Lord until He comes. This is why I can be confident when the weakness of the flesh and of sin seems to crush me. Through Him who was crucified, all is changed: darkness into light, death into life, weakness into strength, emptiness and loneliness into fullness and closeness to You. Through that sacrament in which our crucified and risen Lord is truly present for me, I pray You, Eternal Father, I, a poor sinner, pray You, Father of Mercies and God of All Comfort: Have mercy on me, O God, according to the great fullness of Your mercy. And my poor heart will praise Your goodness for ever.

Amen.

# GOD OF MY LIFE

I should like to speak with You, my God, and yet what else can I speak of but You? Indeed, could anything at all exist which had not been present with You from all eternity, which didn't have its true home and most intimate explanation in Your mind and heart? Isn't everything I ever say really a statement about You?

On the other hand, if I try, shyly and hesitantly, to speak to You about Yourself, You will still be hearing about *me*. For what could I say about You except that You are *my* God, the God of my beginning and end, God of my joy and my need, God of my life?

Of course You are endlessly more than merely the God of my life—if that's all You were, You wouldn't really be God at all. But even when I think of Your towering majesty, even when I acknowledge You as someone Who has no need of me, Who is infinitely far exalted above the lowly valleys through which I drag out the paths of my life—even then I have called You once again by the same name, God of my life.

And when I give praise to You as Father, Son, and Holy Spirit, when I confess the thrice holy mystery of Your life, so eternally hidden in the abysses of Your Infinity that it leaves behind in creation no sign that we could make out by ourselves, am I not still praising You as the God of my life? Even granting that You had revealed to me this secret of Your own inner life, would I be able to accept and realize this mystery if *Your* life had not become *my* life through grace? Would I be able to acknowledge and love You, Father, and You, Eternal Word of the Father's Heart, and You, Spirit of the Father and the Son, if You had not deigned to become through grace the triune God of my life?

But what am I really saying, when I call You *my* God, the God of my life? That You are the meaning of my life? The goal of my wanderings? The consecration of my actions? The judgment of my sins? The bitterness of my bitter hours and my most secret joy? My strength, which turns *my own* strength into weakness? Creator, Sustainer, Pardoner, the One both far and near? Incomprehensible? God of my brethren? God of my fathers?

Are there any titles which I needn't give You? And when I have listed them all, what have I said? If I should take my stand on the shore of Your Endlessness and shout into the trackless reaches of Your Being all the words I have ever learned in the poor prison of my little existence, what should I have said? I should never have spoken the last word about You.

Then why do I even begin to speak of You? Why do You

torment me with Your Infinity, if I can never really measure it? Why do You constrain me to walk along Your paths, if they lead only to the awful darkness of Your night, where only You can see? For us, only the finite and tangible is real and near enough to touch: can You be real and near to me, when I must confess You as Infinite?

Why have You burnt Your mark in my soul in Baptism? Why have You kindled in me the flame of faith, this dark light which lures us out of the bright security of our little huts into Your night? And why have You made me Your priest, one whose vocation it is to be with You on behalf of men, when my finiteness makes me gasp for breath in Your presence?

Look at the vast majority of people, Lord—and excuse me if I presume to pass judgment on them—but do they often think of You? Are You the First Beginning and Last End for them, the One without whom their minds and hearts can find no rest? Don't they manage to get along perfectly well without You? Don't they feel quite at home in this world which they know so well, where they can be sure of just what they have to reckon with? Are You anything more for them than the One who sees to it that the world stays on its hinges, so that they won't have to call on You? Tell me, are You the God of *their* life?

I don't really know, Lord, if my complaint is just or not—who knows the heart of another person? You alone are the reader of hearts, O God, and how can I expect to understand the heart of another when I don't even understand my own? It's just that I can't help thinking of those others, because—as You well know, since You see into the depths of my heart, O Hidden God from whom nothing is hidden—often enough I feel in myself a secret longing to be like them or, at least, to be as they seem to be.

O Lord, how helpless I am when I try to talk to You about Yourself! How can I call You anything but the God of my life? And what have I said with that title, when no name is really adequate? I'm constantly tempted to creep away from You in utter discouragement, back to the things that are more comprehensible, to things with which my heart feels so much more at home than it does with Your mysteriousness.

And yet, where shall I go? If the narrow hut of this earthly life with its dear, familiar trivialities, its joys and sorrows both great and small—if this were my real home, wouldn't it still be surrounded by Your distant Endlessness? Could the earth be my home without Your far-away heaven above it?

Suppose I tried to be satisfied with what so many today profess to be the purpose of their lives. Suppose I defiantly determined to admit my finiteness, and glory in it alone. I could only begin to recognize this finiteness and accept it as my sole destiny, because I had previously so often stared out into the vast reaches of limitless space, to those hazy horizons where Your Endless Life is just beginning.

Without You, I should founder helplessly in my own dull and groping narrowness. I could never feel the pain of longing, nor even deliberately resign myself to being content with this world, had not my mind again and again soared out over its own limitations into the hushed reaches which are filled by You alone, the Silent Infinite. Where should I flee before You, when all my yearning for the unbounded, even my bold trust in my littleness, is really a confession of You?

What else is there that I can tell You about Yourself, except that You are the One without whom I cannot exist, the Eternal God from whom alone I, a creature of time, can draw the strength to live, the Infinity who gives meaning to my finiteness? And when I tell You all this, then I have given myself my true name, the name I ever repeat when I pray in David's Psalter, *"Tuus sum ego."* I am the one who belongs not to himself, but to You. I know no more than this about myself, nor about You, O God of my life, Infinity of my finiteness.

What a poor creature You have made me, O God! All I know about You and about myself is that You are the eternal mystery of my life. Lord, what a frightful puzzle man is! He belongs to You, and You are the Incomprehensible—Incomprehensible in Your Being, and even more so in Your ways and judgments. For if all Your dealings with me are acts of Your freedom, quite unmerited gifts of Your grace which knows no "why," if my creation and my whole life hang absolutely on Your free decision, if all my paths are, after all, Your paths and, therefore, unsearchable, then, Lord, no amount of questioning will ever fathom Your depths—You will still be the Incomprehensible, even when I see You face to face.

But if You were not incomprehensible, You would be inferior to me, for my mind could grasp and assimilate You. You would belong to me, instead of I to You. And that would truly be hell, if I should belong only to myself! It would be the fate of the damned, to be doomed to pace up and down for all eternity in the cramped and confining prison of my own finiteness.

But can it be that You are my true home? Are You the One who will release me from my narrow little dungeon? Or are You merely adding another torment to my life, when You throw open the gates leading out upon Your broad and endless pain? Are You anything more than my own great insufficiency, if all my knowledge leads only to Your Incomprehensibility? Are You merely eternal unrest for the restless soul? Must every question fall dumb before You, unanswered? Is Your only response the mute "I will have it so," that so coldly smothers my burning desire to understand?

But I am rambling on like a fool—excuse me, O God. You have told me through Your Son that You are the God of my love, and You have commanded me to love You. Your commands are often hard because they enjoin the opposite of what my own inclinations would lead me to do, but when You bid me love You, You are ordering something that my own inclinations would never even dare to suggest: to love *You*, to come intimately close to You, to love Your very life. You ask me to lose myself in You, knowing that You will take me to Your Heart, where I speak on loving, familiar terms with You, the incomprehensible mystery of my life. And all this because You are Love Itself.

Only in love can I find You, my God. In love the gates of my soul spring open, allowing me to breathe a new air of freedom and forget my own petty self. In love my whole being streams forth out of the rigid confines of narrowness and anxious self-assertion, which make me a prisoner of my own poverty and emptiness. In love all the powers of my soul flow out toward You, wanting never more to return, but to lose themselves completely in You, since by Your love You are the inmost center of my heart, closer to me than I am to myself.

But when I love You, when I manage to break out of the narrow circle of self and leave behind the restless agony of unanswered questions, when my blinded eyes no longer look merely from afar and from the outside upon Your unapproachable brightness, and much more when You Yourself, O Incomprehensible One, have become through love the inmost center of my life, then I can bury myself entirely in You, O Mysterious God, and with myself all my questions.

Love such as this wills to possess You as You are—how could it desire otherwise? It wants You Yourself, not Your reflection in the mirror of its own spirit. It wants to be united with You alone, so that in the very instant in which it gives up possession of itself, it will have not just Your image, but Your very Self.

Love wants You as You are, and just as love knows that it itself is right and good and needs no further justification, so You are right and good for it, and it embraces You without asking for any explanation of why You are as You are. Your "I will have it so" is love's greatest bliss. In this state of joy my mind no longer tries to bring You forcibly down to its level, in order to wrest from You Your eternal secret, but rather love seizes me and carries me up to Your level, into You.

When I abandon myself in love, then You are my very life, and Your Incomprehensibility is swallowed up in love's unity. When I am allowed to love You, the grasp of Your very mystery becomes a positive source of bliss. Then the farther Your Infinity is removed from my nothingness, the greater is the challenge to my love. The more complete the dependence of my fragile existence upon Your unsearchable counsels the more unconditional must be the surrender of my whole being to You, beloved God. The more annihilating the incomprehensibility of Your ways and judgments, the greater must be the holy defiance of my love. And my love is all the greater and more blessed, the less my poor spirit understands of You.

God of my life, Incomprehensible, be my life. God of my faith, who lead me into Your darkness—God of my love, who turn Your darkness into the sweet light of my life, be now the God of my hope, so that You will one day be the God of my life, the life of eternal love.

# GOD OF KNOWLEDGE

How many things have passed through my brain in the course of my life, O my God! How many things have I thought and learned!

Not as though I now knew them all. I have learned much because I had to, much because I wanted to, but in either case the end result was always the same: I forgot it again. It slipped away from me because our poor, narrow human minds simply cannot take in and hold one thing without letting another sink into oblivion. Or maybe it slipped away because in the very learning of it, there was a hidden indifference which prevented its becoming anything more than another object of bored acceptance and eventual forgetting.

At any rate, most of what I have learned, I have learned in order to forget it again and thus to experience concretely, even in the area of knowledge, my own poverty, narrowness, and limitation. No, that *in order to* is no grammatical mistake or flaw in logic. For look, Lord: if the forgetting were only a tragic mishap and not the true and proper end of all my learning and knowledge, then I would have to desire to know everything I had ever learned.

What a horrible thought! I would still have to retain all the things that were ever crammed into me in all the subjects I ever studied at school. I would still know everything I had ever heard in idle conversations, all I had ever seen in foreign lands or gawked at in museums. And what good would it all do me? Would I be any richer, any more developed or refined?

How could I ever retain it all, anyway? Would it be all stored up in memory like items in a warehouse, to be taken down from the shelf every time an order came in? Or, in the ideal case, would all these items of knowledge be consciously present to me at once?

But how could this vast, confused swarm of knowledge possibly be of any use to me? What would I ever need it for? To make use of it all, I should have to live my whole life over again, right from the first glimmer of consciousness.

O God, it's good to forget. In fact, the best part of most of the things I once knew is precisely the fact that they could be forgotten. Without protest, they have sunk gently and peacefully out of sight. And thus they have enabled me literally to see through them in all their inner poverty and ultimate insignificance.

It is said—and who am I to dispute it, Lord?—that knowing belongs to the highest part of man, to the most properly human of all his actions. And You Yourself are called *"Deus scientiarum Dominus,"* the Lord God of all knowledge. But doesn't such high praise contradict the experience of Your holy writer? "I applied my mind to a new study; what meant wisdom and learning, what meant ignorance and folly? And I found that this too was labor lost; much wisdom, much woe; who adds to learning, adds to the load we bear" (Ecclus 1:17–18).

It is also said that knowing is the most interior way of grasping and possessing anything. But actually it seems to me that knowing touches only the surface of things, that it fails to penetrate to the heart, to the depths of my being where I am most truly "I."

Knowledge seems more like a kind of pain-killing drug that I have to take repeatedly against the boredom and desolation of my heart. And no matter how faithful I may be to it, it can never really cure me. All it can give me is words and concepts, which perform the middleman's service of expressing and interpreting reality to me, but can never still my heart's craving for the reality itself, for true life and true possession. I shall never be cured until all reality comes streaming like an ecstatic, intoxicating melody into my heart.

Truly, my God, mere knowing is nothing. All it can give us is the sad realization of its own inadequacy. All it can tell us is that through it we can never fully grasp reality and make it a living part of ourselves.

How can we approach the heart of all things, the true heart

of reality? Not by knowledge alone, but by the full flower of knowledge, love. Only the experience of knowledge's blooming into love has any power to work a transformation in me, in my very self. For it is only when I am fully present to an object that I am changed by meeting it. And it is only in love that I am fully present—not in bare knowing, but in the affection engendered by knowing. Only then is my knowledge anything more than a fleeting shadow, passing across the stage of consciousness. Then I have knowledge which is really myself, which abides as I myself abide.

Only knowledge gained through experience, the fruit of living and suffering, fills the heart with the wisdom of love, instead of crushing it with the disappointment of boredom and final oblivion. It is not the results of our own speculation, but the golden harvest of what we have lived through and suffered through, that has power to enrich the heart and nourish the spirit. And all the knowledge we have acquired through study can do no more than give us some little help in meeting the problems of life with an alert and ready mind.

Thanks to Your mercy, O Infinite God, I know something about You not only through concepts and words, but through experience. I have met You in joy and suffering. For You are the first and last experience of my life. Yes, really You Yourself, not just a concept of You, not just the name which we ourselves have given You! You have descended upon me in water and the Spirit, in my baptism. And then there was no question of my contriving or excogitating anything about You. Then my reason with its extravagant cleverness was still silent. Then, without asking me, You made Yourself my poor heart's destiny.

You have seized me; I have not "grasped" You. You have transformed my being right down to its very last roots and made me a sharer in Your own Being and Life. You have given me Yourself, not just a distant, fuzzy report of Yourself in human words. And that's why I can never forget You, because You have become the very center of my being.

Now that You live in me, my spirit is filled with something more than pale, empty words about reality, words whose tremendous variety and prolific confusion serve only to perplex and weary me. In baptism, Father, You have spoken Your Word into my being, the Word that was before all things and is more real than they are, the Word in which all reality and all life subsists, endures, and has its being.

This Word, in which alone is life, has become my experience through Your action, O God of Grace. Of Him I shall never tire, because He is one and yet infinite. He can never become tedious or boresome to me, because He is eternal. He draws my spirit away from constant change and inconstancy into a realm of peace, where I experience the ever-old and ever-new possession of everything in one.

Your Word and Your Wisdom is in me, not because I comprehend You with my understanding, but because I have been recognized by You as Your son and friend. Of course, this Word, born as it is out of Your own Heart and marvelously spoken into mine, must still be explained to me through the external word that I have accepted in faith, the "faith through hearing" of which St. Paul speaks.

Your living Word is still shrouded in darkness. It still echoes ever so faintly from the depths of my heart, where You have spoken it, up into the foreground of consciousness, where my scrawny knowledge is wont to parade and take itself so seriously. This is the knowledge that ends in despondency and agony of soul, that brings nothing but the bitter experience of being forgotten and of deserving to be forgotten, because it can never produce living, organic unity. And yet, behind all this labor and torment there is already another "knowledge," which has become in me grace-filled reality: Your Word and Your Eternal Light.

Oh, grow in me, enlighten me, shine forth ever stronger in me, eternal Light, sweet Light of my soul. Sound out in me ever more clearly, O Word of the Father, Word of Love, Jesus. You've said that You have revealed to us all You have heard from the Father. And Your word is true, for what You have heard from the Father is You Yourself, O Word of the Father. You are the Word which knows Itself and the Father. And You are mine, O Word beyond all human words, O Light before whom all earthly light is only night's blackness.

May You alone enlighten me, You alone speak to me. May all that I know apart from You be nothing more than a chance traveling companion on the journey toward You. May it help to mature me, so that I may ever better understand You in the suffering that it brings me, as Your holy writer has predicted. When it has accomplished this, then it can quietly disappear into oblivion.

Then You will be the final Word, the only one that remains, the one we shall never forget. Then at last, everything will be quiet in death; then I shall have finished with all my learning and suffering. Then will begin the great silence, in which no other sound will be heard but You, O Word resounding from eternity to eternity.

Then all human words will have grown dumb. Being and knowing, understanding and experience will have become one and the same. "I shall know even as I am known"; I shall understand what You have been saying to me all along, namely, You Yourself. No more human words, no more concepts, no more pictures will stand between us. You Yourself will be the one exultant word of love and life filling out every corner of my soul.

Be now my consolation, O Lord, now when all knowledge, even Your revelation expressed in human language, fails to still the yearning of my heart. Give me strength, O God, now when my soul easily tires of all the human words we devise about You, words which still fail to give us the possession of You. Even though the few flashes of light I receive in quiet moments quickly fade out again into the dark-grey sky of my daily life—even though knowledge comes to me now only to sink back again into oblivion, still Your Word lives in me, of which it is written: "The Word of the Lord abides forever."

You Yourself are my knowledge, the knowledge that is light and life. You Yourself are my knowledge, experience, and love. You are the God of the one and only knowledge that is eternal, the knowledge that is bliss without end.

# GOD OF MY PRAYER

I should like to speak with You about my prayer, O Lord. And though it often seems to me that You pay little heed to what I try to say to You in my prayers, please listen to me carefully now.

O Lord God, I don't wonder that my prayers fall so short of You—even I myself often fail to pay the least bit of attention to what I'm praying about. So often I consider my prayer as just a job I have to do, a duty to be performed. I "get it out of the way" and then relax, glad to have it behind me. When I'm at prayer, I'm at my "duty," instead of being with You.

Yes, that's my prayer. I admit it. And yet, my God, I find it hard to be sorry for praying so poorly. How can a man hope to speak with You? You are so distant and so mysterious. When I pray, it's as if my words have disappeared down some deep, dark well, from which no echo ever comes back to reassure me that they have struck the ground of Your heart.

Lord, to pray my whole life long without hearing an answer, isn't that too much to ask? You see how I run away from You time and time again, to speak with men who give me an answer, to busy myself with things that give me some kind of response. You see how much I *need* to be answered. And yet, my prayers never receive a word of reply. Or should I say that the interior motion that comes to me in prayer, the occasional light I receive in meditation, is Your word, Your enlightenment? This, of course, is the pat and ready answer which pious writers are so eager to give. But I find it very hard to believe. Again and again I find only myself in all these experiences, only the empty echo of my own cry, when it's Your word, You Yourself, that I want to hear.

I and my ideas are at most useful to me for the sake of others, even when these ideas concern You, and when people think they're quite profound. I shudder at my "profundity," which is really only the flatness of a human being, and a very ordinary one at that. And an "inwardness" in which one finds only himself leaves the heart even more empty than any dissipation or abandonment to the idle bustle of the world.

I find myself endurable only when I can forget myself, when I can get away from myself by prayer and find life in You. But how can I do this if You never show Yourself to me, if You remain ever so distant? Why are You so silent? Why do You enjoin me to speak with You, when You don't pay any attention to me? Isn't Your silence a sure sign that You're not listening?

Or do You really listen quite attentively, do You perhaps listen my whole life long, until I have told You everything, until I have spoken out my entire self to You? Do You remain so silent precisely because You are waiting until I am really finished, so that You can then speak Your word to me, the word of Your eternity? Are You silent so that You can one day bring to a close the life-long monologue of a poor human being, burdened by the darkness of this world, by speaking the luminous word of eternal life, in which You will express Your very Self in the depths of my heart?

Is my life really no more than a single short aspiration, and all my prayers just different formulations of it in human words? Is the eternal possession of You Your eternal answer to it? Is Your silence when I pray really a discourse filled with infinite promise, unimaginably more meaningful than any audible word You could speak to the limited understanding of my narrow heart, a word that would itself have to become as small and poor as I am?

I suppose that's the way it is, Lord. But if that is Your answer to my complaint—in case You should choose to answer me at all—then I am ready with still another objection, and this one comes from an even more anguished heart than my complaint at Your silence, O my distant God.

If my life is supposed to be one single prayer, and my praying is to be a part of this life carried on humbly in Your presence, then I must have the power to present my life, my very self before You. But this is completely beyond my strength.

When I pray, my mouth does the speaking and, if I am praying "well," my thoughts and will-acts obediently play their required, well-memorized little rôle. But is it I myself who constitute the object of the prayer? After all, I'm not supposed to be praying just words or thoughts or will-acts, but *myself*—I should be putting my "self" into my prayer. Even my will belongs far too much to the surface of my soul, and is far too weak to penetrate into those deep levels of my being where I am really "I," where the hidden waters of my life rise and fall according to their own unique law.

What little power I have over myself! Do I really love You when I *want* to love You? Love is a complete pouring out of oneself, a total clinging from the last depths of one's being. Is this what I mean when I say I want to love You?

How can I pray with love, when the prayer of love is the absolute surrender of the heart from its deepest roots, the throwing open of the inmost sanctuary of the soul? I don't have the strength even to budge the heavy gates of this sanctuary—I can only stand helpless and feeble before the ultimate mystery of myself, a mystery which lies buried, immovable and unapproachable, in depths beyond the reach of my ordinary freedom.

I know, my God, that my prayer need not be enthusiastic and ecstatic to succeed in placing me so much in Your power and at Your disposal that nothing is held back from You. Prayer can be real prayer, even when it is not filled with bliss and jubilation or the shining brilliance of a carefree surrender of self. Prayer can be like a slow interior bleeding, in which grief and sorrow make the heart's-blood of the inner man trickle away silently into his own unfathomed depths.

It would be all right if I could pray in this way, or in that other way, if I were just able to give You in prayer the only thing You want: not my thoughts and feelings and resolutions, but myself. But that's just what I am unable to do, because in the superficiality of the ordinary routine into which my life is cast, I am a stranger even to myself. And how can I seek You, O distant God, how can I give myself up to You, when I haven't even been able as yet to find myself?

Be merciful to me, my God. When I flee from prayer, it's not that I want to flee from You, but from myself and my own superficiality. I don't want to run away from Your Infinity and Holiness, but from the deserted marketplace of my own soul.

Every time I try to pray, I am doomed to wander in the barren wastes of my own emptiness, since I have left the world behind, and still cannot find my way into the true sanctuary of my inner self, the only place where You can be found and adored.

Doesn't Your loving sympathy make You understand that, when I am shut out from the place where You live and banned to the marketplace before Your cathedral, I unfortunately fill up this market with the busy distractions of the world? Doesn't Your mercy make You understand that the empty clatter of these distractions is far sweeter to me than the grim and forbidding stillness when I try to pray? This awful quiet is the sole result of my futile efforts at prayer, since I deliberately shut out the noises of the world, and yet I am still hopelessly deaf to the eloquent sounds of Your silence.

What shall I do? You have commanded me to pray, and how can I believe that You have commanded something impossible? I believe that You have given me the order to pray and that I can carry it out with Your grace. And since that's so, the prayer that You require of me must be ultimately just a patient waiting for You, a silent standing by until You, who are ever present in the inmost center of my being, open the gate to me from within. In this way I shall be able to enter into myself, into the hidden sanctuary of my own being, and there, at least once in my life, empty out before You the vessel of my heart's-blood. That will be the true hour of *my* love.

Whether this hour comes in a time of "prayer" in its ordinary meaning, or in some other hour of decision affecting my soul's salvation, or at the time of my death—whether it will be clearly recognizable as *the* hour of my life or not—whether it will last a long time or only a moment—all that is known to You alone. But I must stand ever ready and waiting, so that when You open the door to the decisive moment of my life—and maybe You'll do it very quietly and inconspicuously—I shall not be so taken

up with the affairs of this world that I miss the one great oppor-
tunity to enter into myself and into You. Then in my trembling
hands I shall hold "myself," that nameless something in which
all my powers and qualities are united as in their source, and
I shall return this nameless thing to You in an offering of love.

I know not whether this hour has already struck in my life.
I only know that its last moment will be the moment of my
death. In that blessed and terrible hour You will still be silent.
You will still let me do all the talking, speaking out my own
self to You.

Theologians call Your silence in such a decisive hour the
"dark night of the soul," and those who have experienced it are
"mystics." These are the great souls who have not merely "lived
through" this hour of decision, as all people must, but have
been able to watch themselves in the process, to be somehow
witnesses of their own reactions.

And after this moment shall have come for me, after the
hour of *my* love, which is shrouded in Your silence, then will
come the endless day of *Your* love, the eternity of the beatific
vision. But for now, since I don't know when my hour is coming, nor whether it has already begun to come or not, I must
just wait in the courtyard before Your sanctuary and mine. I
must empty it of all the noise of the world, and quietly endure
the bitter silence and desolation thus produced—the terrible
"night of the senses"—in Your grace and in pure faith.

This, then, is the ultimate meaning of my daily prayers, this
awful waiting. It's not what I feel or think of in them, not the
resolutions I make, not any superficial activity of my mind and
will that You find pleasing in my prayer. All that is only the
fulfillment of a command and, at the same time, the free gift
of Your grace. All that is only clearing the ground, so the soul
will be ready for that precious moment when You offer it the

possibility of losing itself in the finding of You, of praying itself into You.

Give me, O God of my prayer, the grace to continue waiting for You in prayer.

# GOD OF LAW

I n Your book it is written of You, O God, that You are Spirit, and Your Holy Spirit is called the Spirit of freedom: "The Lord is Spirit; and where the Spirit of the Lord is, there is freedom" (2 Cor 3:17). And this is said of You not in the sense that You reign absolutely free and sovereign in the boundless expanses of Your own life, but in the sense that You are *our* spirit and *our* life.

O God of Freedom, our God, it sometimes seems to me that we believe this truth of You because we feel ourselves bound to it by the law of faith. We acknowledge You as our God of freedom because we must, and not so much because the sweeping exuberance of Your Life has filled our hearts, and Your rushing Spirit, who blows wherever He will, has made us free.

Are You truly the Spirit of freedom in my life, or are You not rather the God of law? Or are You both? Are You perhaps the God of freedom through law? Your laws, which You Yourself have given us, are not chains—Your commands are commands of freedom. In their austere and inexorable simplicity they set us free from our own dull narrowness, from the drag of our pitiful, cowardly concupiscence. They awaken in us the freedom of loving You.

Your commands are also truth, since they order us to put first things first, and forbid us to enthrone baseness upon the altar of our life. And since they are truth, they set us free, these commands which You Yourself have given in the New Covenant, or rather have left to us when You abrogated the Old Law, when Christ "freed us unto freedom" (Gal 5:1). Now nothing more remains for us but "the law of freedom" (Jas 2:12). Your commandments may be hard, but they set us free.

But, Lord, what of the commandments imposed upon us by human beings, issued in Your name? Let me tell You quite frankly what rumbles through my heart when the spirit of criticism and discontent is upon me, O God of freedom and of sincere, open speech. I can tell You with confidence—You listen indulgently to such things.

Lord, You have abrogated the Old Law, "which neither our fathers nor we have been able to bear" (Acts 15:10). But You have established rulers in this world, both temporal and spiritual, and sometimes it seems to me that they have diligently set about patching up all the holes that Your Spirit of freedom had torn in the fence of rules and regulations by His liberating Pentecostal storm.

First there are the 2414 paragraphs of the Church's law-book. And even these haven't sufficed: how many *"responsa"* to inquiries have been added to bring joy to the hearts of the jurists! And then there are several thousand liturgical decrees clamoring for our attention. In order to praise You in the Breviary "in psalms and hymns and spiritual songs," in order to "sing and make melody in the heart" (Eph 5:19), I need a road map, a *directorium*, so intricate and elaborate that it requires a new edition every year!

Then there are also various "official bulletins" in the Kingdom of Your Holy Spirit, not to mention countless files, inquiries, replies, reports, decisions, meetings, citations, instructions from every kind of Congregation and Commission. And how resourceful the moralists are at asking tricky questions, until all the pronouncements of all higher authorities are neatly ordered and interpreted.

And what delicate calculations must go into the granting of an indulgence! Only recently some learned theologians found occasion to dispute whether a sick person is obliged to kiss the crucifix of Your Son fourteen times or six times, or fewer, in order to gain an indulgence. What incredible zeal Your servants and stewards have shown in Your absence, during the long period while You have been away on Your journey into the distant silence of eternity! And yet, according to Your own word, where the Spirit of the Lord is, there is freedom.

I don't mean to accuse them, Lord, these wise and faithful servants whom You have placed over Your household. Rather I must say to their praise that they are usually not vulnerable to the reproach which Your Son once made against the Scribes and Pharisees who sat upon the chair of Moses (Matt 23:4). Unlike those rulers and teachers of old, Your modern stewards have imposed heavy burdens not only on others, but on themselves too.

Generally speaking, Lord, Your household of the laity has only Your sweet yoke and Your light burden to carry, belief in Your Word, Your own commandment that frees us unto love, and the burden of Your grace flowing from the sacraments. And if this yoke weighs heavily upon us, then it's only because we're weak and our hearts are evil, so that we should actually complain against ourselves and not against Your yoke. The burden about which I was complaining in the stillness of my heart is mainly *our* burden, the burden of Your priests, which we have actually picked up and set upon our own shoulders.

But isn't it still a real burden? Or is it only Your kind of freedom, which seems heavy and constraining to our narrow, petty, comfort-seeking hearts? Is it only the excess weight of Your grace? There is perhaps no more enlightened or enlightening answer to this question than that given by Your Son. He has told us that Your lower servants should do and observe all that Your higher servants have commanded them, and that those to whom You have given power to bind and loose must one day give an accounting to You, as to whether their binding was always really a releasing of their brethren into the realm of Your true freedom (Matt 23:3).

I know, and I hope that this knowledge will grow ever stronger and more vital in me, that Your freedom can never be won through protest against the authorities who derive their power from You. We can transform that weighty power into Your buoyant freedom only by doing what is right, only by using it as "Your minister for good" (Rom 13:3-4).

When I am really honest with myself, I recognize time and time again that it is not Your Holy Spirit of freedom that makes this burden so vexing, but the unholy spirit of my own love of comfort, my own self-will and self-seeking. I rise up in rebellion because I will not take the trouble to have consideration for my brother, to avoid scandalizing him, even though I know that Your Son shed His Blood for him; because I want to consider everything that is clean as allowed; because I have knowledge which puffs up, and not the charity which edifies (Rom 14:13ff.; 1 Cor 8:1ff.).

And haven't I often called things barriers and restrictions upon Your freedom, when they were actually a defensive wall for the protection of the liberty of loving You, a safeguard against the law in my own members? How many times have I learned through hard experience that the human laws of Your Church are a salutary school of patience and discipline, of self-mastery and self-possession, of consideration and love of neighbor?

How often have I found out that we grow to maturity not by doing what we like, but by doing what we should? How true it is that not every *should* is a compulsion, and not every *like* is a high morality and true freedom. Conscious willing is found even in infants, but consciously accepted obligation is the sign of a mature man. O grant that I may not always belong to the class of the infants who continually want to play the game differently, who are never satisfied with the rules as they are!

I know too that all the detailed rules and regulations, the ceremonies and customs, methods and tricks of the trade which are commanded, or at least recommended to me, can be made the external expression of my interior love, provided of course that I have the love. I know that these things are dead weight only when I myself am too weak and lifeless to put my heart into them.

Your Church, O my God, has to be visible. Only thus is she the "vessel of the Holy Spirit," as Irenaeus called her. And if she is to be visible, if Your Spirit is to become ever more visible and tangible in her, then she must express herself in commandments and customs, in "yes and no," in "here and now," in "thus and not otherwise." And he who grasps all this with a believing heart and a vigorous love, enters through the narrow gate of the commandments into the broad expanse of Your Spirit.

O my God, I have talked much to prove my good will toward the many commandments and orders, and the even more numerous prohibitions of the spiritual authorities that You have set over me. I want to observe all that they have commanded. And this will definitely be a blessing to me. But what of You Yourself: are You the God of these laws?

Obviously You want me to keep them: that much is clear. And it's also clear that, in order to understand Your will properly, we must keep in mind several of the things that the moralists say at the beginning of their books about norms of interpretation, causes excusing from culpability, canonical equity, etc. But are You really the God of such laws?

It's hard for me to make clear, even to myself, what I mean by this question. Let me put it this way: in the commandments which You Yourself have given, it's almost as if You were actually present. You have made them Your commandments, precisely because that which they contain is the expression of Your own Holiness and Goodness, because we would be unlike You if we did not love what You command. Our rejection of Your commandments would be ultimately a rejection of You Yourself.

But it's not like that in the case of the laws originating from human authority. The prescribed cut of the clerical gown in itself has nothing to do with the Holiness of Your Being—I can serve You as a priest no matter how long or short a cassock I wear. You are not present in that law, just as You would not be present in its opposite. Why, then, must I seek You in precisely this way, when You could just as well be found in another?

Is it because the authorities You have placed over me have so ordered? Yes, of course. But why must they order precisely this? Because the unbounded realm of the possible can be reduced to living actuality only by a more or less arbitrary choice? Because otherwise, if everyone were free to choose according to his own arbitrary judgment, there would arise disorder and hopeless confusion? Yes, that may often enough be the reason. But is it the reason always and in every case? Can all the laws and regulations of Your Kingdom be considered merely as necessary ordinances ensuring order and uniformity, as mere concrete determinations of Your own Law? Are they only spiritual traffic laws?

If they were no more than this, then they would constitute no burden to our inner, personal freedom. No one can seriously claim that his personal liberty is unduly restricted by traffic

laws. But what of the other laws, which are not simply concrete expressions of Your own Law, and yet are something
more than mere external regulations governing the area of
interpersonal relations? What of these, which affect me inte-
riorly, in my own personal being and its freedom?

I am not asking You whether I should obey these laws—the
answer to that question is perfectly clear to me—but rather
how I can obey them in such a way that I meet You in them.
It's true: they require my interior compliance, and not just
external fulfillment, since they govern my inner self, directing
the personal actions of the real "me." And yet they are not like
Your own commandments, for when I obey these, I can be confident that my subjection to the law is *eo ipso* an act of devotion to You.

I always feel that, if one is not careful, he can easily become
a mere fulfiller of the law, doing what is commanded externally
and quite apathetically. He can turn into a "legalist," an anxious,
slavish worshiper of the letter of the law, who thinks he has
fulfilled all justice before You when he has fulfilled the human
ordinance. Such a man mistakes the letter of the law for You
Yourself.

I don't want to be a legalist, nor a mere servant of men, nor
a servant of the dead letter. And still I must fulfill the commands of human superiors. I want to observe their ordinances
with all my heart, but I can't see how I can give my heart
completely to such an object. The inner man should obey such
laws, and yet he should not be a slave of men.

Thus, the only answer seems to be that, whenever I obey
such a law, I must keep looking directly at You. In this way I
can pay homage to You, directly and exclusively, and not to the
thing that is required of me, not even to the thing as the
reflected splendor of Your Being. Precisely because there is in
the thing itself nothing to which I can give my heart without

reserve, obedience can be the expression of my seeking You alone in it.

Thus, in obedience to such human regulations, either I don't find You at all, or I find You and You alone, according as I obey out of pure love of You or not. In Your own commandments You are present even when we obey them without intending our obedience as an act of love of You, because their very content is necessarily an expression of Your sacred Being. But in the commandments of human superiors we find nothing but a human will, and thus, instead of making us free, they take away freedom, unless we obey them out of love of You.

If I look upon my obedience to these human laws as a demonstration of homage for Your beloved free Will, which rules over me according to its own good pleasure, then I can truly find You therein. Then my whole being flows toward You, into You, into the broad, free expanse of Your unbounded Being, instead of being cramped within the narrow confines of human orders. You are the God of human laws for me, only when You are the God of my love.

Give me a ready and willing heart, O Lord. Let me bear the burden of the commands issued by Your authorities in such a way that this bearing is an exercise of selflessness, of patience, of fidelity. Give me Your Love, which is the only true freedom, the love without which all obedience to human authority is mere external observance and servitude. Give me a heart filled with reverence for every legitimate command, and also respect for the freedom of Your children, which You have won for me by Your own redeeming obedience.

May the kingdom of Your freedom come! It is the kingdom of Your Love, and it is only there that I am truly free from myself and from the will of my fellow men, because there I am not serving them, nor for their sakes, but serving You, for Your sake.

In no command do I belong to men, but to You, and he who belongs to You is free. You are not the God of laws because You will that we should serve the law: You are rather the God of the one law, that we should give our love and service to You alone.

And I pray also, as You wish me to pray, for all superiors You have placed over me, that their commands may never be anything else but the appearance and fulfillment on earth of the one great law of loving You.

# GOD OF MY LORD JESUS CHRIST

You are the Infinite, my God, the Limitless Being. Everything that is and can be is eternally present to You. Whatever I come to know has had its home in Your Mind from all eternity. Whatever I desire, You have always possessed. Whatever I love is fundamentally what Your Love has already eternally embraced, You Yourself. You are Wisdom, Power, Goodness, Life, and Strength. You are everything I can ever long for or imagine.

But how can You be all those things together? Here where I make my abode, the things that men know and love and long for are always separate, alienated from each other, dismembered. Things are limited—they have some qualities, but not others. Thought is pale and lifeless; goodness lacks power; power is without love; uncontrolled vitality turns deadly and brutal.

We never succeed in compressing together into the narrow confines of our finiteness everything that appears good to us, good just because it is: life and wisdom, goodness and power, strength and tenderness. These and all the other varied forces of our life are things we neither can nor want to do without, and yet each of them inevitably excludes another. There is only one thing we can do, and do it we must: order all these forces, arrange them in some kind of hierarchy, allot to each of them its proper place and limits, so that no single one becomes complete master and thus blots out all the others. We must preserve "order" in our life, we must live a life of "moderation."

We must be careful lest the spirit become the adversary of the soul, lest goodness turn into weakness, lest strength degenerate into mere brute force. All these things are like so many parasites clamoring for a share of our life's-blood, all greedily desiring to live in us and through us. And we must play the rôle of the thrifty housewife, parceling out our limited energy among them in tiny little measuring-cups.

There is nothing here into which we dare throw ourselves completely, nothing to which we can fully abandon ourselves. Any such lack of moderation would spell ruin both for us and for the object of our attachment. Those who know everything are seldom warm of heart; the mighty of this world are usually hard; and it is proverbial that the beautiful are often stupid. And so it must be: how could we be finite and be all these things together?

But where is All-Wisdom, which is also Eternal Love? All-Power, which remains All-Good? Pulsing Vitality, which is just as fully Living Spirit? Beauty, which is Vibrant and Wise? Where can these elements of greatness grow without limit, spread themselves irresistibly unto infinity? Where can they flourish and develop in such a way that each still remains entirely compatible with everything else, in fact, is actually identified with everything else, instead of pushing all the rest out of existence?

That Being is You, my God. You are all in all, and in everything that You are, You are all. Each separate quality that we attribute to You as something absolutely boundless, instead of driving all other qualities out of the very realm of possibility, rather gives them all limitless space for development.

In You knowledge so expands itself to Omniscience that it becomes Omnipotence, and the frightening inexorableness of Your Omnipotence turns into the irresistible force of Your Goodness. All that is cramped and confined, oppressed and imprisoned in the narrowness of my finite being, becomes in You the one Infinity, which is both Unity and Infinity combined. Each of Your attributes is of itself Your whole immeasurable Being; each carries in its bosom the whole of reality. Thus, of all the things man can love, there is at least one which he can love without limit and unconditionally, without need for "order" and "moderation," and that is You.

In loving Your holy Immensity, our ordinary life of enforced moderation and proportion becomes tolerable. In You the heart can safely follow its yearning for the limitless, can wander aimlessly without going astray. I can prodigally lavish my affections on every single aspect of Your Being, and find in each of them everything I seek, because everything in You is the whole.

When we find our way to You on this path of love, then the burden of our finiteness is mercifully lifted from us, at least for the moment while such love lasts. And then we can come back to our dull daily routine and be satisfied again with the restrictions of our smallness.

Your Infinity, O God, is thus the salvation of our finiteness. And yet I must confess that the longer I think about You, the more anxious I become. Your Awful Being threatens my security, makes me lose all sense of direction. I am filled with fear and trembling because it often seems to me that Your Infinity, in which everything is really one and the same, is meant for You alone.

Obviously Your whole Being is present in each of Your attributes and in each of Your deeds. And You are also wholly present when You come down upon me, when You break into the circle of my life. You don't have to take any special measures to make sure that the lightning-stroke of Your Omnipotence, when it flashes across my life's horizon, is also the soft, gentle light of Your Wisdom.

You can channel Your whole Being into the torrent of Your Power, and all is still under control: the rushing waters have not gone beyond the limits You intended, have not released any new potentiality of which You Yourself are not the perfect fulfillment. You can be an inexorable tribunal of justice, and to Your ear a sentence of eternal damnation is still a hymn of joy praising Your immeasurable Goodness. But to me and my smallness that very thought brings terror—it makes me feel that all my joints are being sundered.

You are always Yourself, whole and entire, no matter how You deal with me. You are always the Infinite Unity of all reality, whether You love me or pass over me, whether Your Power or Your Goodness, Your Justice or Your Mercy are revealed in me. But precisely because You are the one Infinity of all being and will always remain so no matter how You manifest Yourself, I am left in agonizing uncertainty. Whenever I think of Your Infinity, I am racked with anxiety, wondering how You are disposed toward me.

When I try to take You into account in the calculations of my life, I can only put You down as an "unknown"—the riddle of Your Infinity, which Itself contains everything, throws all my calculations off, and so the end result is still an insoluble puzzle. How can I use Your Goodness as a factor in my reckoning, when Goodness in You means also a holy severity? How can I add in Your fathomless Mercy, when it is also Your inexorable Justice? With this one word You tell me everything: Infinity. But it is precisely this word that renders futile all attempts at neatly planning out my life. You are thus the eternal threat in my life, frightening me out of all sense of security.

No, Lord, You must speak to me in a word that does not mean everything at once, a word that does not embrace the whole of reality in one unfathomable unity. You must say a word to me that means just one thing, one thing which is not everything. You must make Your infinite word finite, if I am to be spared this feeling of terror at Your Infinity.

You must adapt Your word to my smallness, so that it can enter into the tiny dwelling of my finiteness—the only dwelling in which I can live—without destroying it. Then I shall be able to understand; such a word I can take in without that agonizing bewilderment of mind and that cold fear clutching my heart. If You should speak such an "abbreviated" word, which would not say everything but only something simple which I could grasp, then I could breathe freely again.

You must make Your own some human word, for that's the only kind I can comprehend. Don't tell me everything that You are; don't tell me of Your Infinity—just say that You love me, just tell me of Your Goodness to me. But don't say this in Your divine language, in which Your Love also means Your inexorable Justice and Your crushing Power—say it rather in *my* language, so I won't have to be afraid that the word *love* hides some significance other than Your Goodness and gentle Mercy.

O Infinite God, You have actually willed to speak such a word to me! You have restrained the ocean of Your Infinity from flooding in over the poor little wall which protects my tiny life's-acre from Your Vastness. Not the waters of Your great sea, but only the dew of Your Gentleness is to spread itself over my poor little plot of earth. You have come to me in a human word. For You, the Infinite, are the God of Our Lord Jesus Christ.

He has spoken to us in human language. No more can the word *love* mean anything that I must fear. For when He says that He loves us, and that in Him You love us, this word comes from a human heart. And to a human heart this word has only one meaning, only one blessed and blissful meaning. If this human heart loves us, the heart of Your Son, the heart which—may You be praised forever!—is finite like my own poor heart, then my heart is at peace. For it loves me, and I know that such a love is only love and nothing else.

Jesus has really told me that He loves me, and His word has come from the depths of His human heart. And His heart is Your heart, O God of Our Lord Jesus Christ. Thus, if this human heart of Your Son is unspeakably richer and greater than my heart, it is so only in that love and that goodness which can never be anything else but love and goodness. It can never conceal within itself the awe-fulness of Your Infinity, which is always all else as well.

Grant, O Infinite God, that I may ever cling fast to Jesus Christ, my Lord. Let His heart reveal to me how You are disposed toward me. I shall look upon His heart when I desire to know Who You are. The eye of my mind is blinded whenever it looks only at Your Infinity, in which You are totally present in each and every aspect at once. Then I am surrounded by the darkness of Your unboundedness, which is harsher than all my earthly nights. But instead I shall gaze upon His human heart, O God of Our Lord Jesus Christ, and then I shall be sure that You love me.

But I have still one more request. Make my heart like that

of Your Son. Make it as great and rich in love as His, so that my brothers—or at least one of them, sometime in my life— can enter through this door and there learn that You love him. God of Our Lord Jesus Christ, let me find You in His heart.


# IN PRAISE OF CREATION


O God, I must confess to myself as well as to You that which has come to me again and again. It is with great difficulty that I behold Your creation as wondrous, although indeed it is. The Scriptures deem Your creation glorious; the poets sing praises to it, Saint Francis, too, in his Canticle of the Sun, of which the final verse about Death still moves me deeply.

I know only too well that it is my own feeling of guilt, my sense of frustration, and the numbness of my spiritual faculty which prevent me from going into raptures over oceans, mountain peaks bedecked with snow, dark, remote forests, the cosmos with its billions of light years and the teeming path of its unfolding. And were I not shaken with revulsion at the mutual greed residing in nature (despite the fact that Saint Paul might forbid me to take for granted the groanings of the whole of creation), I would still have to confess with sincere regrets that neither am I acutely aware of, nor can I instinctively feel, the true glory of Your creation, of nature itself. It is enough for me to behold Your creation through my eyes, my ears, and my nostrils, in which my heart ought and should forever rejoice, yet I see that my heart does not burst with joy. A sign of old

age perhaps, which withers and allows all things to fade?
Should I be patient with myself or rather force myself into
joining that chorus of poets who extol the power, the sublim-
ity, the infinite mercy and the awful splendor of Your creation,
and therefore have an inkling of who You truly are?

> Praised be You, my Lord,
>     with all Your creatures,
> And most of all with that exalted woman,
>     our sister sun,
>         who brings forth the day and who gives us light.
> Fair and radiant in majestic splendor
>     is she, Your very image, O exalted One!

> Praised be You, my Lord,
>     through brother moon and the stars.
> You have formed them on the Heavens,
>     shining, exquisite, and lovely.

> Praised be You, my Lord,
>     through brother wind, through air and cloud,
>     through fair as through all weather.
> All creatures You have enlivened through them!

> Praised be You, my Lord,
>     through sister water.
> She is so fruitful, modest, fine, and chaste.

> Praised be You, my Lord,
>     through brother fire.
> Through him You brighten the dark night,
>     so fair is he, so serene, powerful, and strong.

> Praised be You, my Lord,
>     through our sister mother earth.
> She nourishes and provides for us
>     and coaxes forth all manner of fruit,
>     colorful flowers, and grass into bloom.

Praised be You, my Lord,
  through our brother death.
No living being can escape him.
Woe to those who perish in sin!
Blessed be those who depart
  in the sanctity of Your holy Will!
The second death cannot harm them.

May You be extolled and praised, my Lord,
  humbly thanked and faithfully served!

One may also pray in whatever tongue is asked of a person. In this way, even my prayer can be heard by You along with the words of Saint Francis, by You, Creator of all things in this noble universe.

  Amen.

# WITH CHRIST

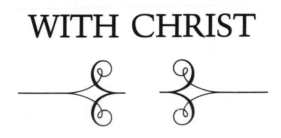

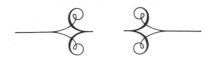

# CHRIST ALL IN ALL

Lord Jesus Christ, Eternal Word of the Father and True Man, we adore You. Be to us ever the living mystery of our faith and of our life which is grounded in our faith. Eternal high priest and continuing sacrifice, be our adoration of Your Father in spirit and in truth. May our life be of service to God everlasting in You and with You, who are the Sacrament of homage paid to the divine majesty.

Life of Humanity, source of grace, be the very life of our souls, the life that makes us sharers in the life of the threefold God. We participate in Your life through You, the Sacrament of the supernatural life of our souls.

Savior of Sinners, Merciful Victor over our sins and our weakness. Our desire is to live in You, so that the strength of Your love, which alone is always with us and all-powerful against sin, may be efficacious in us. Preserve us from sin, through You and in You, the Sacrament of victory over all sin.

Bond of Love, Symbol of Concord. Unite me in Yourself through all those whom You have bidden me love. Grant that we may all belong to You more and more. In this way we will be united with one another in love more and more, through You, the Sacrament of true love and communion.

Victor over Suffering, Crucified Redeemer. In You we will surmount the difficulties of all our hours of darkness. Whatever may befall us, may we bear it as a share in Your destiny and may it be for us a path into the eternal Easter light, through You, who are the Sacrament of the communion of suffering, which we share with You.

Lord of eternal glory, may we always be ready, full of faith and courage, to enter into Your eternal life. When we receive You, may Your body be to us the pledge of eternal glory. O Sacrament of Eternal Life, grant that we may be given our heart's last desire: to see You at last face to face and to adore You with the Father and the Holy Spirit for ever.

Amen.

# PRAYER AT CHRISTMAS

God, the Eternal Mystery of our Life, by the birth of Your own word of love in our flesh You have made the glory of Your life in its eternal youth into our life, and have caused it to appear in triumph. Grant us that when we experience the disappointments of our lives we may be enabled to believe that Your love, which You Yourself are and which You have bestowed upon us, is the eternal youth that is our own true life.

# REFLECTION ON THE PASSION

L ord Jesus Christ, our Savior and Redeemer, I kneel before Your blessed cross. I want to open my spirit and my heart to contemplate Your holy sufferings. I want to place Your cross before my poor soul that I might know it a little better, that I might receive more deeply into my heart all that You did and suffered, and that I might realize who it was for whom You suffered. May Your grace be with me, the grace to shake off the coldness and indifference of my heart, to forget my everyday life for at least this half-hour, and to dwell with You in love, sorrow, and gratitude. King of All Hearts, may Your crucified love embrace my poor, weak, tired, and discouraged heart. fill my heart with an interior awareness of You. Stir up in me what I need so badly: compassion for You, love for You, honesty and fidelity, and perseverance in the contemplation of Your holy sufferings and death.

I want to meditate upon Your seven last words upon the cross, the last words You spoke before You entered into the silence of earthly death. You Who are the Word of God from eternity to eternity. You spoke them with parched lips and out of an anguished heart, those words which came straight from Your heart at the very end. You spoke them to everyone. You spoke them even to me. Let them penetrate into my heart. Right to its very core. Right to its very center. That I might understand them. That I might never again forget them. That they might live in me and become the strength of my lifeless heart. Speak them Yourself to me, so deeply that I feel Your voice vibrating within me.

You will be speaking to me someday at the moment of my

death, and even after my death. Those words will be either an eternal beginning, or an everlasting end for me. O Lord, let me hear words of mercy and love from You at the moment of my death. I shall not ignore those words. Let me, therefore, here and now open my heart to receive Your last words upon the cross.

# THE SEVEN LAST WORDS

*Father, forgive them,*
*For they know not what they do.*
Luke 23:34

You are hanging upon the cross. You nailed Yourself to it. You are not going to come down any more from this pole suspending You between heaven and earth. Your body aches from its many wounds. The crown of thorns is tormenting Your head. Blood is running down into Your eyes. The wounds in Your hands and feet burn as though Your limbs were pierced with a white-hot iron. And Your soul is a sea of sorrow, anguish, and hopelessness.

Those who prepared all this for You stand there beneath the cross. They will not even go away and let You die alone. They stand around. They laugh. They decide that they were right, that the very condition You are in is the clearest proof that what they did to You has satisfied divine justice. They have rendered to God a service of which they should be proud. And so they laugh. They mock. They blaspheme.

A feeling of despair at the sight of such wickedness comes over You, a feeling more terrible than all the pain in Your body. Are there men capable of such wickedness? Do You have anything in common with such men as this? Can one man torture another to death like this? Torture him to death with lies, wickedness, treachery, hypocrisy, and malice, and yet keep up the appearance of righteousness, the air of innocence, the pose of impartial judges? Does God let this happen in His world? Can Satan, laughing and sneering, force his way into God's world so jauntily and so sure of victory? O Lord, in such a situation our hearts would have been crushed under the weight of terrible despair. We would have fled from the devil, and from God too. We would have cried out, and frantically pulled at the nails with our hands so that we could once again clench our fists in anger.

But You said: "Father, forgive them, for they know not what they do." You are really a mystery, O Jesus. Where in all Your tortured and tormented soul did You find a place for words like these? Yes, You are a mystery. You love Your enemies. You recommend them to Your Father. You pray for them. And my Lord, if it is not blasphemous to say it, You pardon them with the most implausible excuse there is: they did not know what they were doing. Really they knew it all. But they did not want to know it! And what a person does not want to know he does know in spite of himself, in the deepest, most hidden recesses of his heart. But he hates this knowledge and so refuses to let it come into the clear light of consciousness. And You say: "They did not know what they were doing." But there is one thing that they really did not know: Your love for them. Only the man who loves You can know Your love for him. For it is only upon the man who gives love that there dawns an understanding of the love he has received.

Speak these merciful words of Your boundless love over my

sins also. Say to the Father in my behalf: "Forgive him, for he did not know what he was doing." Really I did know it. I knew all of it. But Your love I did not know.

Let me also recall Your first word on the cross when I thoughtlessly mention in the Our Father that I forgive those who have committed wrongs against me. O my God hanging on the cross, if anyone really has wronged me, I am not sure that I could forgive him. And so I need Your strength to pardon and forgive with all my heart those whom in my pride and selfishness I consider my enemies.

Forgiveness of others in time of suffering.

> *Amen I say to you*
> *This day you will be*
> *With Me in Paradise.*
> Luke 23:43

You are now in the agony of death, Your heart is filled to the brim with anguish, and yet You still have a place in that heart for the sufferings of another. You are at the point of death, and yet You are concerned about a criminal, who even in his agony must admit that the hellish pangs of his death are but the just punishment for his evil life. You see Your Mother standing there, but You speak first to the prodigal son. A feeling that God has abandoned You is oppressing You, but You speak of paradise. Your eyes are growing dark in the night of death, but they still see the light of eternity. In death, man's only concern is with himself, for then he is all alone, all by himself. But Your concern is with the souls that are going to enter Your kingdom with You. How merciful is Your heart! How strong and courageous it is!

A miserable criminal asks You to remember him. And You promise him paradise. Is everything going to be different after

You die? Will a life of sin and vice be transformed this quickly when You draw near it? When You speak the words of transformation over a life, will even the sins and hateful wickedness of a criminal's life be so transformed by grace that there is nothing left to keep him from approaching the all-holy God?

Surely we too would have admitted some small measure of good will in a robber and criminal like him. But evil habits and vicious instincts, brutality, filth, and meanness, all these do not vanish because of a little good will and a passing feeling of regret in someone on the gallows. Such a man does not enter heaven as quickly as penitents and people who have purified themselves for a long time, people like the saints who have only to sanctify their bodies and souls and make them worthy of the thrice-holy God. But You utter the all-powerful word of Your grace and it goes straight to the heart of this robber. It transforms the hell-fire of his death-agony into the purifying flame of divine love. This divine love transfigures in an instant all that remains of the work of the Father, and consumes all the evil and guilt that keeps God from entering his heart.

Will You also give me the grace never to lose the courage to be bold enough to ask and expect anything from Your goodness? The courage to say, even if I were the most condemned criminal: "Lord, remember me when You come into Your kingdom." O Lord, let Your cross be set up at my deathbed. And let Your lips say to me also: "Amen I say to you, this day you will be with Me in paradise." This word itself would make me worthy to enter the kingdom of Your Father, render me completely forgiven and sanctified by the purifying power of a death in You and with You.

*Woman, behold your son;*
*Son, behold your Mother.*
John 19:26

Now, at the hour of death, the moment has come when Your Mother should again be with You. Now is not the time for her to ask You for a miracle, but it is the time for You to die, and so she should be there. For she was the one to whom You said: "Woman, what do You want Me to do? My hour is not yet come." Now the hour is come, and the Son and the Mother will share it. This is the hour of farewell, the hour of dying. This is the hour when the Mother, who is a widow, is to lose her only Son.

And so once again Your eyes glance down to Your Mother. You have spared this Mother nothing. You were not only the joy of her life, but also the bitterness and suffering of her life. But both of these were Your grace, for both were Your love. And because in both she stayed at Your side and served You, You love her. Not until she did this was she really Your Mother in the fullest sense. For Your brothers and sisters and Mother are they who do the will of Your Father Who is in heaven.

Even here in Your agony Your love is quick to express the tenderness which in this world every son feels for his mother. And through Your death even the tender, precious things of our world such as this are consecrated and sanctified, these things which make the heart gentle and the earth beautiful. They do not die in Your heart even when it is being crushed in death. And so they are redeemed for heaven. There will be a new earth because even in death You loved the earth, because even while dying for our eternal salvation You were touched by the tears Your Mother was shedding, because even while giving up Your life so that the earth could be made whole You were anxious about a widow, and gave a son to a mother and a mother to a son.

But she does not stand there beneath Your cross merely with the lonely sorrow of a mother whose son is being put to death. She stands there also in our name. She stands there as the Mother of all the living. She gives up her Son in our behalf. It was in our name that she spoke her *"fiat"* to the death of the Lord. She was the Church under the cross; she was the race of the children of Eve; she was fighting the whole world's struggle between the serpent and the Son of the woman. And so, if You gave this Mother to the disciple whom You loved, You gave her to all of us.

You are saying also to me: "Son, daughter, behold Your Mother." O word that gave us a legacy that will last forever! Only the man who takes Your Mother as his own from that hour can stand under Your cross, O Jesus, as the disciple whom You love. And all the grace merited by Your death comes to us through the pure hands of this Mother. Say to her as You look upon my poor soul: "Woman, behold your son; Mother, behold your daughter."

Only a pure, virgin heart like the heart of this Mother could have given its consent in the name of the whole world to the marriage of the Lamb with its bride, the Church, the whole human race purchased and purified by Your blood. If I let myself be entrusted by You to the heart of Your Mother, Your death will not be lost on me. And then I shall be present to see the day of Your eternal nuptials dawn, that day when all creation will be made new and united with You forever.

*My God, My God,*
*Why have You forsaken Me?*
Matthew 27:46

D eath is drawing ever closer. I do not say the end of life on this earth, for that is salvation and peace. But death, and death is the ultimate depths, the unimaginable depths of destruction and agony. Death is drawing near, and death is emptiness, terrible weakness, crushing solitude. In death everything disintegrates, everything slips away, and only forsakenness remains, a forsakenness full of pain and yet unspeakably numbing.

In this night of the senses and of the spirit, in this desert that consumes everything in Your heart, Your soul is still in prayer. The dreadful wasteland of a heart devastated by suffering becomes in You a solitary call to God. O Prayer of Anguish, Prayer of Abandonment, Prayer of Unfathomable Weakness, Prayer of a Forsaken God, let us adore You. If You prayed like this, O Jesus, if You prayed in such an agony, is there any abyss so deep that we cannot call out from it to Your Father? Is there any despair so hopeless that it cannot become a prayer by being encompassed within Your abandonment? Is there any anguish so numbing that it must no longer expect its mute cries to be heard amidst heaven's jubilation?

To express Your anguish, to utter the prayer of Your total abandonment, You began to say the twenty-first psalm. For Your words: "God, My God, why have You forsaken Me?" are the first verse of this ancient lamentation which Your Holy Spirit Himself once put into the heart and upon the lips of a holy man of the Old Testament to express his anguish. And so, if I dare speak this way, the only prayer that You wanted to say during this most bitter agony was one that had been prayed thousands and thousands of years ago. In a sense You prayed in the words of the liturgy when You offered Your own solemn Mass, that Mass in which You offered Yourself as an eternal sacrifice. And in those words You were able to say everything that had to be said. Teach me to pray in the words of Your Church in such a way that they become the words of my own heart.

*I thirst.*
John 19:28

J ohn the Evangelist, who heard this word himself, says this about it: "Knowing that everything was now accomplished, that the Scripture might be fulfilled. You said: 'I thirst.'" Here too You have made Your own a verse from the Psalms which the Spirit of God uttered in prophecy about Your future sufferings. For the same twenty-first Psalm says of You: "My throat is dry as a potsherd and My tongue sticks to My jaws." And in Psalm 69:22 it says of You: "In My thirst they gave Me vinegar to drink."

O Servant of the Father, obedient unto death, even the death of the cross, You look at everything that is happening to You, and then at what is supposed to be happening to You; at everything You are doing, and then at what You should be doing; at all the actual events and then at what should be. Even here in the agony of death, which usually darkens the spirit and prevents any clear reflection, You are in a sense anxiously concerned that everything in Your life be in harmony with the eternal image that exists in the mind of the Father when He thinks of You.

And so in saying these words Your real concern is not the nameless thirst of Your body that is now bleeding to death and covered with burning wounds, naked and exposed to the scorching, Oriental sun at mid-day. You are telling us, rather, that even here in death, with an almost incomprehensible humility that demands our worship, You are faithful to the will of the Father: "Yes, even what the lips of the prophet foretold of Me as the will of the Father is fulfilled. Yes, truly I thirst." O Noble Heart, for You even the senseless fury of the pain tormenting Your body is but the fulfillment of Your mission from above.

But You have approached all Your suffering with all its terrible severity with this same attitude. It was a mission, not blind fate. It was the will of the Father, not the wickedness of men. It was the saving act of Your love, not the deed of sinners. You were lost that we might be saved; You died that we might live; You thirsted that we might find refreshment in the waters of life. You were tormented by thirst that from the heart in Your pierced side there might flow streams of living water. You invited all to come to this heart when You cried out with a loud voice on the feast of tabernacles: "If anyone thirst, let him who believes in Me come to Me and drink. For from the heart of the Messiah shall flow streams of the living waters of the spirit."

You thirsted for me. You thirsted after my love and my salvation: as the deer thirsts for the spring, so does my soul thirst for You.

*It is finished.*
John 19:30

Y ou really said: "It is fulfilled." Yes, Lord, Your end has come. The end of Your life. The end of Your honor, the end of Your human hope, the end of Your struggle and labor. Everything is over and done. Everything has been emptied out.

Your life has run its course. You are hopeless and powerless. But this end is Your fulfillment. For whoever comes to the end in love and fidelity has reached fulfillment. Your failure is Your triumph.

O Lord, when shall I once and for all grasp this, this law of Your life and so of my life? The law that death is life, losing oneself is finding oneself, poverty is riches, and suffering is a grace, that to reach the end in truth is fulfillment.

Yes, You have reached fulfillment. The mission that Your Father gave You is fulfilled. The chalice that was not to pass from You has been drunk. The death that was so terrible has been endured. The redemption of the world is accomplished. Death is conquered. Sin is vanquished. The power of the spirit of darkness is broken. The gateway to life is open. The freedom of the sons of God is won. The quickening Spirit of grace can now breathe where He will. Already the horizon of this dark world is slowly beginning to grow red as the dawn of Your love breaks upon it. And in only a little while—the little while that we call the history of the world—it will burst into flame, the clear flame of the fire of Your Godhead. And then the whole world will be plunged into the flaming sea of Your love. All is finished.

Bring me to fulfillment in Your Spirit, You Who brought the whole world to completion, Who are the Word of the Father Who brought all things to fulfillment by becoming flesh and accepting its torments.

Shall I too be able to say someday in the twilight of my life: "It is finished; I have accomplished the mission You gave me to do"? When the shadows of death fall upon me, shall I be able to pray after You the words of Your high-priestly prayer: "Father, the hour is come . . . I have glorified You on earth by accomplishing the work You gave Me to do. And now, Father, do Thou glorify Me with Thyself"? O Jesus, may the mission the Father has given me be whatever He wants it to be—great or small, sweet or bitter, life or death. Grant that I might accomplish it as You did. For You have already brought everything to completion, including my life, so that I can complete it.

> *Father, into Your hands*
> *I commend My spirit.*
> Luke 23:46

O Jesus, utterly forsaken, tormented by suffering, You have come to the end. To that end where everything is taken away, even one's soul and his freedom to say "yes" or "no," and hence where man is taken from himself. For that is what death is. Who or what does the taking? Nothing? Blind fate? Merciless nature? No, it is the Father! God, Who is wisdom and love! And so You let Yourself be taken from Yourself. You give Yourself over with confidence into those gentle, invisible hands. We who are weak in faith and fearful for our own selves experience those hands as the sudden, grasping, merciless, stifling grip of blind fate and of death. But You know that they are the hands of the Father. And Your eyes, now grown dark in death, can still see the Father. They look up into the large, peaceful eyes of His love, and from Your lips come the last words of Your life: "Father, into Your hands I commend My spirit."

You give everything to Him Who gave everything to You. You put everything into the hands of Your Father without guarantee and without reservations. That is doing a great deal, and it is a hard and bitter thing to do. All alone You had to bear the burden of Your life: all men, their meanness, Your mission, Your cross, failure and death. But now the time for enduring is past. Now You can put everything and Yourself into the hands of the Father. Everything. Those hands are so gentle and so sure. They are like the hands of a Mother. They embrace Your soul as one would lift a little bird carefully and lovingly into his hands. Now nothing is difficult any more, everything is easy, everything is light and grace. And everything is safe and secure in the heart of God, where one can cry all his anguish out, and the Father will kiss away the tears from the cheeks of His child.

O Jesus, will You one day put my poor soul and my poor life also into the hands of the Father? Put everything there, the burden of my life, and the burden of my sins, not on the scales of justice, but into the hands of the Father. Where should I flee, where should I seek refuge, if not at Your side? For You are my brother in bitter moments, and You suffered for my sins. See, I come to You today. I kneel beneath Your cross. I kiss the feet which follow me down the wandering path of my life constantly and silently, leaving bloody footprints behind.

I embrace Your cross, Lord of Eternal Love, Heart of All Hearts, Heart that was pierced, Heart that is patient and unspeakably kind. Have mercy on me. Receive me into Your love. And when I come to the end of my pilgrimage, when the day begins to decline and the shadows of death surround me, speak Your last word at the end of my life also: "Father, into Your hands I commend his spirit." O good Jesus.

Amen.

# THE PRESENCE OF JESUS AND HIS LIFE

L ord Jesus Christ, Son of the Living God, True God and True Man, One Person in two distinct but undivided natures, we adore You because You are truly present here with us.

You are present here first of all because You are God from all eternity, of one being, one power, and one majesty with the eternal Father, present in all things and all places because of Your infinity, in which all things live and move and have their being.

And You are also present here as man. You are here with us in the Sacrament of the Altar with Your body and soul and with Your human heart. You are present in the Sacrament, You Who were born of the Virgin Mary, lived a human life, and accepted whatever that life brought: the big things and the little things, the joys and the tears, the long, monotonous routine and the moments of greatness. You are present in the Sacrament, You Who suffered under Pontius Pilate and were crucified. You are present in the Sacrament. You Who drank the chalice of suffering to the very dregs on the cross. You are present in that body which was brought back to life and glorified with God's own majesty. You are with us in Your human heart which now experiences the joy of all eternity, and in Your human spirit which now gazes upon the inaccessible light of the Father and His Son and His Holy Spirit, and sees the eternal, Trinitarian God face to face.

You are truly present here as man. When we look, we do not see anything, but the eye of faith sees You, and sees You as our brother, present here with us. When we listen, we do not hear anything, but the ear of faith catches the sound of the eternal hymn of praise which You as High Priest sing to the eternal Father in behalf of all men, a hymn that You will sing forever from a heart now joyful and filled with the glory of God.

We adore You, we praise You, we thank You, we give glory to Your majesty because You wanted to dwell among us, You Who are our God, Who are our origin and our beginning, our end and our destination. We thank You because You wanted to dwell among us as a man just like ourselves. We thank You because You wanted to be born as we are born, to make Your way as a pilgrim through the narrow confines of our creature-liness and through the valley of our tears, and to reach Your end and destination by going through all this as we must do, You Who are the end and destination of all things.

You are present with us. And hence Your human life is present with us, closer to us than we can imagine. Seen in their deepest reality, all the things that made up Your life nineteen hundred years ago are only apparently past. To be sure, the earthly surface of Your life is past. You will never again be born as a poor child, now You never get hungry and thirsty. You never get tired. You never cry. The multicolored, everchanging nothingness that we call human life does not pass by You any more as it once did, no longer courses through Your soul to change You and to leave its mark on You. You do not die any more. All that is over and past for You, and its value lies precisely in its being unique and transitory. All these things are past now, for even that part of You which is human, created, finite, and mutable has passed over into the eternity of the Father, has reached the goal that is its fulfillment, where all change reaches its fulfillment in what is final and definitive. It is there that reality is freest and most alive, where the whole course of time is drawn up into the single "now" of eternity which encompasses everything in a single instant. Your temporal, human life is past, but in becoming past it has passed over into God.

And for this reason it remains present in its deepest reality. For Your human life is now perfectly united with the eternal God Who is the origin of all things and in Whose wisdom and love everything past is eternally and unalterably present. Your human spirit and Your human heart see and embrace Him in Whom all time has its eternity, all becoming its everlasting permanence, all change its endless stability, and the whole past its eternal present. In the eternal wisdom and love of God Himself Your heart continually sees and loves, acknowledges and embraces the presence of Your past life in God, for in God that life has its fullest presence.

But also in Your heart itself, O Jesus, Your past life is still present in a very real sense.

For what passes in a human life is merely the external event. But when this event sinks into the darkness of past nothingness, it gives birth to something eternal. It contributes its part to the formation of the spiritual person in us, and that person is eternal. In the passage of time there comes to be in us something that does not pass away. We are not like a street, on which the endless stream of moments passes and then is just as empty as it ever was, once the moments have passed. We are much more like a storehouse, in which every moment leaves something behind as it passes, namely that part of it which is eternal: the uniqueness of a free act of love, the finality of a person's decision for or against God. For these are timeless realities. It is as though the waves of time break silently against the shores of eternity in their constant ebb and flow, and as though every wave, every moment, every deed leaves behind that part of itself which is eternal: its goodness or its evil. For these are the eternal elements in the things of time.

This eternal goodness or evil of our past actions sinks down into the eternal ground of our soul, penetrates into it, and gives shape to the hidden core of our soul. It is hidden from us, of course, not from God. And so there is gradually formed in the passage of time something eternal, the countenance of our soul that is to last forever, and in that countenance our eternal destiny is decided. When time reaches the end of its course, everything is not really over and done with. For then the waters of transitoriness are merely drained off, leaving behind and revealing to the eyes of man what had been hidden: his life as he has freely formed and fashioned it for its eternal existence.

So it is also with You, O Jesus, for You are truly a man. You really lived a human life. And so this whole life remains present in You as well as in God. You are at this moment and forever the person that You came to be throughout the course of Your life. Your childhood is past, but You are still at this moment a person Who has lived through a childhood. You are now what only someone Who was once a child can be. Your tears are dried up, but You are now what only someone can be Who has once cried, Whose heart can never forget the reasons for its tears. Your sufferings are past, but the maturity of a man Who has suffered is Yours forever. Your earthly life and death are past, but what came to be through them exists for all eternity, and so is present with us. The courage of Your life which overcame all things has an eternal presence, and so does the love which animated and transfigured Your life. Your heart and its response of total surrender to the incomprehensible will of the Father has an eternal presence, and also Your obedience, Your fidelity, Your meekness, and Your love for sinners. All of these grew and became strong through all the moments of Your life, and, because You freely embraced them, they have entered into the structure of Your real and permanent human self. It is as this person that You are now with us, and so everything that You were and lived and suffered are also present with us.

There is still a third reason why the life that You once lived is present here with us in a very real sense. When You lived Your life on earth, You did not know and love only Your own earthly surroundings, Your own country, and the people who were Your contemporaries. You also knew and loved all of us, and this not only as God, but also in Your human heart. You knew and loved even me, my life, my times, my surroundings, my destiny, my moments of greatness and littleness, all that I have freely chosen to be. You already had a knowledge of all of this in the mysterious interiority at the center of Your being. You had already taken all of this into Your heart and borne it there. And so my life had a share in the formation of Your life. My life belongs to Your destiny. During Your life You had already acknowledged my life. You prayed for me, You cried for me, You gave thanks for the graces I was to receive. Because during Your life You were deeply concerned about me, Your attitude toward me and my life forms part of the reality of Your life. And when Your life entered into eternity and then became present with us in this Sacrament, it gave You a presence with us precisely as the person Whose life, now in its final state, had always included knowledge of me and love for me.

It is as this person that we wish to adore You. O Jesus, we adore You. O Eternal God, we adore You.

Our Redeemer, present here in this Sacrament, we adore You.

Jesus, present as true man, we adore You.

Life and death of Jesus, present from all eternity in the immutable knowledge and will of the eternal Father, we adore You.

Life and death of Jesus, present for all eternity in Your heart which became what it is now, and will be forever in heaven, through this life and death, we adore You.

Life and suffering of Jesus, truly present with us whose lives You already knew and loved during Your life and suffering, we adore You.

Jesus, Who are truly present with us, we adore You.

# THE PRESENCE OF JESUS' AGONY IN THE GARDEN

Jesus, You are truly here with us. You are with us as man, in flesh and blood, in heart and spirit. And so Your human life is also present here with us, for it is not simply past, but has entered into the eternal reality of Your heart.

And so the hours of Your struggle and suffering in the Garden of Olives are also present with us, and it is these hours that we want to honor in faith and love, in sincerity and gratitude, with compassion and reparation during this hour.

In the glory of heaven Your human spirit sees even at this moment the Father's eternal, immutable will which appointed for You to live the hours in the Garden of Olives. Your heart is still adoring this will of the Father even now. And Your spirit and Your heart are present with us.

You are with us, You Who endured the agony in the Garden. What You lived through and suffered then is now past: no longer do sadness and anguish, the bitterness and the agony of death touch Your heart, now that it has entered upon the blessedness of the Father. But Your heart is the heart that it is because of what it experienced and suffered then, and all this experience and suffering remain in it. It is with this heart that You are present with us. The Apostle says of You in Hebrews 5:7 that in the days of Your earthly life, with a loud cry and tears, You offered up prayers and supplications to Him Who was able to save You from death, and that You learned obedience from the things that You suffered. It is as this person that we now adore You, and we say to You Who became what You are through Your agony in the garden: have mercy on us.

O Jesus, in the obedience that You learned in the Garden of Olives, have mercy on us.

Jesus, in the resignation that You won by Your struggle in the Garden, have mercy on us.

Jesus, in Your readiness to suffer that was tried and proven in the Garden of Olives, have mercy on us.

Jesus, in Your love for us that was not overcome in the Garden of Olives, have mercy on us.

Jesus, in Your goodness that was not embittered even in the Garden of Olives, have mercy on us.

Jesus, in Your courage that remained steadfast even in the Garden of Olives, have mercy on us.

Jesus, in Your meekness that did not falter even in the Garden of Olives, have mercy on us.

Jesus, in the anguish and sorrow of those hours, have mercy on us.

Jesus, in Your fear and trembling, have mercy on us.

Jesus, in the prayer that You offered in the Garden of Olives, have mercy on us.

Jesus, Who fell prostrate on the ground, have mercy on us.

Jesus, Who persevered in prayer again and again, have mercy on us.

Jesus, Whose soul was sad even unto death, have mercy on us.

Jesus, Who prayed that the chalice of suffering might be taken away, have mercy on us.

Jesus, Who said: "Not My will, but Thine be done," have mercy on us.

Jesus, Who cried: "Abba, Father," have mercy on us.

Jesus, Who three times said "yes" to the will of the Father, have mercy on us.

Jesus, Who was abandoned by the sleeping apostles, have mercy on us.

Jesus, Who was comforted by an angel, have mercy on us.

Jesus, Who suffered a bloody sweat in Your agony in the Garden of Olives, have mercy on us.

Jesus, Who knew and suffered in advance all future sufferings, have mercy on us.

Jesus, Who knew the sins of the whole world in the Garden of Olives, have mercy on us.

Jesus, Who felt disgust at the sins of all ages, have mercy on us.

Jesus, Who knew my sins in the Garden of Olives, have mercy on us.

Jesus, Whose heart was saddened by my sins in the Garden of Olives, have mercy on us.

Jesus, Who was willing to take all this upon Yourself in the Garden of Olives, have mercy on us.

Jesus, Whose heart was grieved by the fruitlessness of Your suffering, have mercy on us.

Jesus, Who felt abandoned by God during Your agony in the Garden of Olives, have mercy on us.

Jesus, Who was obedient to the incomprehensible will of the Father, have mercy on us.

Jesus, Whose love for God never wavered though He seemed only to be angry, have mercy on us.

Jesus, Who in the Garden of Olives prayed for all who would ever suffer, have mercy on us.

Jesus, Who in the Garden of Olives was the most abandoned of all the abandoned, have mercy on us.

Jesus, Who in the Garden of Olives spoke for all who cry out to God from their anguish, have mercy on us.

Jesus, Who in the Garden of Olives set an example for all who suffer temptation, have mercy on us.

Jesus, Who in the Garden of Olives gave comfort to all who struggle painfully in the agony of death, have mercy on us.

Jesus, Who in the Garden of Olives was the head of all who must suffer for the sins of the world, have mercy on us.

Jesus, Who in the Garden of Olives shared as a brother in the distress and despair of the whole world, have mercy on us.

Jesus, Who in the Garden of Olives understood all suffering, have mercy on us.

Jesus, Who in the Garden of Olives offered a haven to all who are forsaken, have mercy on us.

Jesus, Who in the Garden of Olives still loved every sinner, have mercy on us.

Jesus, Who in the Garden of Olives still wanted to press to Your heart the most condemned, have mercy on us.

Jesus, Whose agony in the Garden of Olives redeemed our death and made it a happy homecoming, have mercy on us.

Jesus in the Garden of Olives, be merciful to us: spare us, O Jesus.

Jesus in the Garden of Olives, be merciful to us: deliver us, O Jesus.

From the sins that You wept for in the Garden of Olives, deliver us, O Jesus.

From ingratitude for Your love, deliver us, O Jesus.

From indifference to Your suffering, deliver us, O Jesus.

From a lack of compassion for Your agony and death, deliver us, O Jesus.

From resistance to the grace that You won for us in the Garden of Olives, deliver us, O Jesus.

From rejecting Your acceptance of suffering and expiation in the Garden of Olives, deliver us, O Jesus.

From doubt about God's love during our own nights in the Garden of Olives, deliver us, O Jesus.

From bitterness over our own bitter agony in the Garden of Olives, deliver us, O Jesus.

From despair in our moments of abandonment, deliver us, O Jesus.

We poor sinners, we pray You, hear us.

Forgive us our sins, we pray You, hear us.

Give us an understanding of Your suffering, we pray You, hear us.

Teach us Your surrender to the will of the Father in the Garden of Olives, we pray You, hear us.

Give us Your perseverance in prayer during the night of Your agony in the Garden, we pray You, hear us.

Give us the dispositions of Your heart during those hours in the Garden of Olives, we pray You, hear us.

Grant us an understanding of penance and reparation, we pray You, hear us.

Let us recognize our suffering as a share in Your holy suffering, we pray You, hear us.

Fill us with Your disgust for our sins, we pray You, hear us.

Give us Your strength and patience in our trials and abandonment, we pray You, hear us.

Let Your courage in the face of death be with us in our own death-agony, we pray You, hear us.

Send us Your consoling angel at the hour of our death, we pray You, hear us.

Teach us to watch and pray with You always in the Garden of Olives, we pray You, hear us.

Teach us to pray when we feel weak and discouraged, we pray You, hear us.

Put into our hearts and upon our lips the name "Father," especially when God seems to be only the Lord, the stern judge, and the incomprehensible, unapproachable God, we pray You, hear us.

Lamb of God, Who takes away the sins of the world, spare us, O Lord.

Lamb of God, Who takes away the sins of the world, hear us, O Lord.

Lamb of God, Who takes away the sins of the world, have mercy on us.

Let us pray: Jesus, Who are present here, as we consider the holy dispositions of Your divine and human heart, those dispositions in which You suffered the agony in the Garden of Olives in reparation, obedience, and love, and with which You dwell among us even now, we say this prayer to You: fill our hearts with sorrow for our sins; let us in union with You take up our crosses in a spirit of penance and reparation; and grant that we may gratefully return the love that You have shown us, that love which prompted You to endure Your most holy sufferings in the Garden of Olives for us sinners.

Amen.

# THE PRESENCE OF THE AGONY IN THE GARDEN IN US

Lord Jesus Christ, You are present here in this holy Sacrament. But this is not the only way that You dwell among us. You also live within us. Ever since we were incorporated by baptism into Your Mystical Body, which is the Church, You live within us by Your Holy Spirit. He has anointed us and sealed us. And so You are the life of our life, the life of our spirit, the life of our heart. In the strength and life-giving power of Your Holy Spirit, Who proceeds from the

Father through You. You have taken hold of the most hidden depths of our soul, the innermost center of our being. You have transformed and glorified it; You have made it holy and divine.

It is no longer we who live, but You Who lives in us. We no longer belong to ourselves. We belong to You. You are the law of our life, the interior strength of our being and our actions, the hidden light of our spirit, the flame that burns in the depths of our heart, the holy splendor of our whole being. We have been transfigured by the eternal light of God Himself.

You exist and live in us; You share Your own being and life with us through Your presence as uncreated Grace; You give us the power through created grace to receive You and the one, Trinitarian God, and thus to live Your life, the life of God. For these reasons we are really and truly sons and daughters of Your eternal Father. By the grace of Your incomprehensible love, we are really Your brothers and sisters, co-heirs with You of the glory of Your Father, that glory which the Father communicates to You as God in His eternal act of generation. He also bestows that glory on Your human soul by grace, just as He bestows it on us. And so we are really filled with that eternal love which proceeds from You and from the Father as the person of the Holy Spirit.

You live in us so very much, O Jesus, that even Your presence in the Sacrament is only the means by which You declare, communicate, increase, and strengthen Your presence in us by grace. Your presence in the Sacrament will last only until the end of time, but Your presence within us will remain forever. As soon as the veil of faith that hides it falls away, Your presence will rise up from those depths of our heart which are hidden from us now, and will then become our eternal life.

But since You live within us, our life is subject to the law of Your life, even down to what are seemingly the smallest details of our life in the world. Our life is a continuation of

Your life. When we were baptized, a new chapter in Your life began; our baptismal certificate is a page from the history of Your life. So we must fashion ourselves after Your image, You Who are the first-born of many brothers. We must even "put You on." Since You live within us, Your image must become more and more manifest in us. God's hidden grace in Your human soul made Your earthly life a pure expression and revelation of itself in the world of earthly phenomena. So too must this same grace—Your grace—make our lives, all that we do and suffer, a revelation of grace, and thus make our earthly life conformed to Your earthly and heavenly life. You wanted to live Your life in every age, in every situation, among all peoples and generations. Since You could not do this within the narrow, created confines of Your own earthly life, You take hold of our lives by Your grace and by Your Holy Spirit. He comes to us through Your pierced heart to try to make our lives like Yours. In this way, O Jesus, Your life lives on in ever new forms and expressions always and everywhere until the end of time.

But if Your life is to express itself anew in our lives by Your grace and by Your Holy Spirit, then this is true even of Your suffering, of Your blessed passion. For this is the decisive event in Your life. In baptism we were baptized into Your death, as the Apostle says. Since we are the children of God, filled with Your Spirit, and co-heirs with You, we must suffer with You and thus win a share in Your glory. The Apostle says that we bear always Your suffering in our body, so that Your life might become manifest in our mortal flesh. Since You are the crucified, it is as the crucified that You must manifest Yourself in us. You continue to suffer in the members of Your Mystical Body until the end of time. Not until the last tear has been shed, the last pain suffered, and the last death-agony endured will Your suffering, O Jesus, really be finished. If Your cross does not weigh also upon me, I cannot be Your disciple. If Your suffering does not become my portion also, I must admit that the spirit and the law of Your earthly life are not dwelling and working in me. And then I would not belong to You. I would be far from You, Who are my true and eternal life.

You want to continue Your sufferings in me for my own salvation and that of the whole world, and for the glory of Your Father. By my sufferings and agony, You want to fill up what is wanting in Your sufferings for Your Body, which is the Church. And so I shall receive in my life again and again a share in Your agony in the Garden of Olives, a very small share, but nevertheless a real one. My "holy hours," those hours when I honor Your agony in the Garden of Olives, will be made in the truest sense not during the peaceful hours of these pious devotions here in church. My real "holy hours" are those hours when sufferings of body and soul come to overwhelm me. Those hours when God hands me the chalice of suffering. Those hours when I weep for my sins. Those hours when I call out to Your Father, O Jesus, and do not seem to be heard. Those hours when faith becomes agonizingly difficult, hope seems to be giving way to despair, and love seems to have died in my heart. They are the real "holy hours" in my life, those hours when Your grace working in my heart draws me mysteriously into Your agony in the garden. When those hours come upon me, O Lord, have mercy on me.

When Your agony in the Garden of Olives overshadows my life, stand at my side. Give me then the grace to realize that those holy hours of Yours are a grace, that they are hours of Your life, of Your agony in the Garden of Olives. And let me understand at that moment that in the final analysis they come upon me not through blind chance, not through the wickedness of men, not through tragic fate. They come rather as the grace to share in Your destiny, which was to suffer in the Garden of Olives.

Give me then the grace to say "yes," "yes" to even the most bitter hours, "yes" to everything, for everything that happens in those hours, even what results from my own guilt, is the will of Him Who is eternal love. May He be blest forever. Give me in those hours the grace to pray, even if the heavens appear leaden and closed, even if the deathly silence of God falls upon me like a tomb, even if all the stars of my life flicker out, even if faith and love seem to have died in my heart, even if my lips stammer out words of prayer which ring as lies in my lifeless heart.

In those hours Your grace is still within me, and may it transform the chilling despair that seeks to destroy my heart into an act of faith in the reality of Your love. In those hours may the annihilating weakness of a soul in its death-agony, a soul with nothing left to cling to, become a cry to Your Father in heaven. In those moments—let me say it while I kneel before You—let everything merge into and be embraced by Your agony unto death in the Garden of Olives.

Have mercy on us, O Jesus, when the angel of our lives hands us the chalice as he handed it to You. Have mercy on us at that moment, but not by taking the chalice away from us. Anyone who belongs to You must drink it with You as You drank it. Rather, have mercy on us by being with us, not to make us feel strong during those hours, but that Your strength might be victorious in our weakness. Have mercy on us, we pray You. During Your agony in the Garden of Olives You saw before You all who would ever suffer through such hours in the Garden, and this sight gave comfort to Your heart. Grant that we might belong to the number of those who were Your consolation in that hour. This is the mercy that we ask of You.

When You share with us the hours of Your Agony in the Garden of Olives, have mercy on us.

When we should recognize the hours of our suffering as a sharing in Your agony, have mercy on us.

When God's will seems difficult and incomprehensible to us, have mercy on us.

When sorrow and sadness, disgust and anguish overshadow us as they did You, have mercy on us.

When sorrow for our sins comes upon us, have mercy on us.

When the holiness and justice of God fills us with terror, have mercy on us.

When we must do penance and make reparation for our failures, have mercy on us.

When we are called upon to share in the sufferings of Your Mystical Body, the Church, have mercy on us.

When we are tempted out of selfishness to exaggerate our suffering and to pity ourselves, have mercy on us.

When we are betrayed by friends as You were, have mercy on us.

When we are left without help as You were, have mercy on us.

When we meet hatred with hostility as You did, have mercy on us.

When our love receives only ingratitude in return, have mercy on us.

When the Father does not seem to hear our prayer, have mercy on us.

When the light of faith seems to be going out during our night of suffering, have mercy on us.

When hope seems to be giving way to despair during our hours in the Garden of Olives, have mercy on us.

When God's love seems to have died in us during our real "holy hours," have mercy on us.

When nothing else lives on in us except our final misery, our complete powerlessness, and the incomprehensibility of God, have mercy on us.

When the agony of death strikes us as it did You, have mercy on us.

Lamb of God, Who took upon Yourself all our suffering in the Garden of Olives, spare us, O Jesus.

Lamb of God, Who redeemed and sanctified our suffering in the Garden of Olives and on the cross, hear us, O Jesus.

Lamb of God, Who accompanies into the glory of the Father all who suffer with You and in You, have mercy on us, O Jesus.

Amen.

# THE ASCENSION AND PRESENCE OF THE LORD

Lord, when You return even as You have departed from us, as a true man, then may You find Yourself in us as the one who bears all, is patient, is faithful, is kind, is selfless; as the one who cleaves to the Father even in the darkness of death, the one who loves, the one who is joyful. Lord, may You find Yourself in us, being what we would so much wish to be yet are not. But Your grace has not only endured. In reality, it has come to us simply in virtue of the fact that You, having ascended and been enthroned at the right hand of God, have poured out Your Spirit into our hearts. And so we truly believe that against all experience You do continue Your life in us even though it seems to be only ourselves—Ah! almost always only ourselves and not You—that we find within ourselves. You have ascended into heaven and are seated at the right hand of God with our life. You are coming back with that life in order to find Your life in ours. And the fact that You will find it there—that will be our eternity even when we, together with all that we are and have lived and have possessed and have borne, shall have entered into the glory of Your Father through Your second coming.

# THE IMITATION OF CHRIST

Lord Jesus Christ, Son of the Living God, we worship You, true God and true Man in one person; God of Eternity, incarnate in our time, and with us all days until the end of time.

You have shared everything with us. You Yourself, glorious and consubstantial reflection of the Father, have lived our life. You know it, this our life, You have experienced and lived it to the full. You know what it is like. We cannot claim that You did not know what it is like to be a man, that You could not feel what it means to be subject to the powers and forces of this earth. You have felt what it is like to have a body, the flesh of sin and death; what it is like to be captive in the limitations imposed by the forces of this world: hunger, death, politics, folly, wretchedness, traditions, laws, all of which are our masters; the obligation to earn one's bread, our involvement in the world around us and in social positions not of our choosing. You were a man. Therefore it must be a meaningful, splendid and happy thing to be a man. Because of You and Your human life we believe this.

You have shared with us, too, all You brought with You to this earth: the love of Your Father, his glory, his divine life, his truth, which is the essential truth of all truth. You have given us everything which the Father gave You: participation in the divine nature, sonship, the Holy Spirit, eternal life. We accept it. We are ready to be infinitely more than mere men: to be the sons of eternity, children of God, heirs of the covenant, Your brothers, temples of Your Spirit, royal priests, who praise Your Father and offer the world back to its creator as a song of praise, workers in Your vineyard, witnesses to Your truth, worshipers in the spirit, heralds of light, shining, as the apostle says, like lights in the midst of a crooked and perverse generation (Phil 2:15).

Come and live within us. Our life and death both belong to You. Let us be subject to Your rule of life. Order us as You will. We will not demur, but assent to Your continuing Your life in us, in the wretchedness of our ordinary everyday life, the life whose very food is Your Father's will. We want to imitate You. Eternal High Priest, we want to continue Your prayer through all ages, until the world can begin the eternal prayer of praise, the eternal Amen to all that God has done. We want to pray during the ordinary days and at the great moments of our lives, in the depths of temptation, in the weakness of our hours in Gethsemane and in the final solitude of our hearts. We beg of You the grace to pray always without ceasing. We ask for Your Holy Spirit, that he may carry our poor words aloft on the wings of his divine language to the threefold life of God, over the abyss of nothingness and out of this world into the infinity of God eternal. We believe that we never pray alone, but that You remain in our midst and Your Holy Spirit within us and pray with us, whether we are praying in the community of Your holy people or alone in our room. Worshipper of the

Father in spirit and in truth, pray in us and with us all the days of our life.

We want to be Your witnesses and Your apostles. Witnesses of Your truth and Your love, envoys of Your mission to save the world. As the Father sent You, so You send us all. Your mission is hard and difficult. We are weak, cowardly and reluctant, headstrong and clumsy. We find our own selves enough of a burden to bear. But nevertheless we want to go forward. We are ready to begin again and again. We will always want to creep away, tired and longing for rest. Do not let us rest. Always keep us on the alert. Teach us that we can only effect our own salvation when we care for that of others. Make us see clearly and act swiftly in the opportunities there are to work for Your kingdom. Give us hope against hope, grant us Your strength in our weakness. Lend us the love that is selfless and patient, trusting and true. Let us not in our apostolate overlook those who are closest to us. If Your Spirit lives in us and inspires us, we can imitate You. Then You are within us, furthering Your own word, the word of mercy, the act of redemption, the transformation of the world.

Whenever we follow You, guided by Your spirit, Your kingdom is brought a little nearer. Now we still live by faith and in affliction beneath the shadow of Your Cross. But it is in this way that Your true kingdom comes, the realm of truth and life, the kingdom of holiness and grace, of justice, love and peace. Give us the grace to follow You and imitate You faithfully.

Amen.

# FOLLOWING CHRIST
# THROUGH LOVE OF NEIGHBOR

Lord Jesus Christ, You Yourself have shown me a way to a faith that is real and determines my life. It is the way of the ordinary and actively generous love of neighbor. I meet You on this road, as unknown and known. Guide me on this path, Light of Life. Let me walk it in patience, always further, always new. Grant me the incomprehensible strength to venture towards people and to give myself in the gift. Then You, Yourself, in an unexplicable union with those who receive my love, step forward to meet me in my neighbor: You are the One Who can take on the whole life of humankind, and You remain at the same time the One in Whom this life, handed over to God, does not cease to be love for humankind.

My faith in You is "on the way" and I say with the man in the Gospel: "I believe; Lord, help my unbelief." Guide me along Your path, You Who are the Way to my neighbor, my unknown, looked-for brother, and therein are God, now and forever.

Amen.

# GOD'S WORD AS PERSONAL PROMISE

Jesus, You asked that boundless, totally revealing and probing question of human existence which I myself am. But this happened not only through words, but through Your entire earthly life, not half-way and with hesitation, as in my case. I, on the other hand, cling to the particular which is safe and prefer a death which I am solely made to endure by death itself as absolute ambiguity, but do not actively participate in. You, of course, died freely, and in You God asked this boundless question as His own, embraced it Himself and raised it up into that answer which is His own blessed incomprehensibility.

What the Church, whose baptized member I am, tells me about You often sounds incomprehensible to me. Teach me through my life what is meant by it. I want to be patient and be able to wait. I will try to translate it for myself over and over again into that which I experience in You. But I shall also broaden and incorporate what I experience into that which Your Church believes and proclaims about You.

You *are* yesterday, today, and in eternity, because Your life cannot have been lost before God. You are the infinite question in which I and my dying life participate, namely, human being. You are the Word of God, because in You God promised Himself to me and spoke Himself as answer. You are God's answer because the question which You are, as the dying Crucified One, has been definitely answered with God, in Your resurrection. You are God-man, both uncommingled and forever undivided. Let me be Yours in life and death.

Amen.

# MEETING JESUS

Jesus, all the Church teaches about You is good and I gladly say over and over again before it: "I believe; Lord, help my unbelief." But the Church's teaching about You is good only because it intends to illuminate my own particular inner perception of You, no, *You Yourself*, as You speak Yourself through Your Spirit into my heart, and as You silently meet me in the events of my life, as the experience of Your indwelling grace.

You meet me, Jesus, in my neighbor towards whom I have to venture without guarantee in that fidelity to conscience which does no longer pay; in all love and joy which is still only promise and asks me for the courage to believe in *eternal* love and joy; in the slow rising of the dark waters of death in the pit of my heart, in the darkness of that death which is a life-long dying in the ordinary way of difficult service in everyday trials; everywhere You meet me, You are in everything, unnamed or called by name. For I search for God in all things in an effort to flee from deadening nothingness, and in all things I cannot abandon the person I am and love. Therefore everything proclaims You, the God-man. Everything calls out to You in Whom as man one already possesses God without once more having to let go of humanity, and in Whom as God one can find humanity without having to fear meeting nothing but the absurd.

I cry out to You. The last strength of my heart reaches out for You. Let me find You, let me meet You in the whole of my life so that slowly I also come to understand what the Church tells me about You. There are only two final words: God and human, one *single* secret to which I totally surrender in hope and love. It is in being twofold that this mystery is truly one, one in You, Jesus Christ. As I put my hand into Your wound I say to You with the doubting and questioning Thomas: "My Lord and my God."

Amen.

# IN THE HOLY SPIRIT

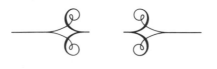

# THE HOLY SPIRIT

Lord Jesus Christ, son of the Father, the goal and the way for us and for all men. Exalted above all Heavens, seated at the right hand of the Father You have poured out upon us the Spirit of the promise, so that You might remain with us in Your Spirit all days unto the end and, through the Spirit, continue in us Your life and death to the glory of the Father and for our salvation.

Lord, see the spirits which trouble us all around; grant us the gift of discriminating between them. Give us the knowledge which will prove its value in our daily longing for You: the knowledge that if we seek for You and long for You, it will be Your Spirit that will bring calm, peace and confidence, freedom and simple clarity; while all spirits of unrest and anxiety, perplexity and heavy depression will come from our own nature or be demons of darkness. Give us the Spirit of Your

comfort. Lord, we know that even in days of despair, barrenness or spiritual weakness we should be true to You, must and
can be true to You. Yet still we pray for the spirit of comfort
and strength, of joy and confidence, of growth in faith, hope
and charity, of cheerful and confident service to the glory of
Your Father, still we pray for the spirit of calm and peace.
Drive from our hearts spiritual despair, darkness and confusion, the inclination towards base and earthly things, mistrust
without hope, indifferences, sadness, feelings of loneliness and
separation, and above all the the suffocating feeling of being far
from You.

But if it is Your will to lead us on such difficult paths, then
we implore You, send us at least during these days and hours
the Holy Spirit of faithfulness, steadfastness and perseverance,
so that we can go forward with blind confidence, holding to our
route and remaining true to the resolutions which we chose
when Your light showed us the path and Your joy enlarged our
hearts. Yes, in the midst of such loneliness give us a spirit of
courage and determination, a spirit to defy our difficulties and
to concentrate more than ever on our prayers, our self-exami-
nation, and our penance. Give us the unconditional confidence
to know that even in these times of loneliness we are not forsaken by Your grace, that undiscerned You are indeed with us,
as the strength which gives our weakness the victory. Give us
a spirit which faithfully recalls the past and Your loving visita-
tions; a spirit which looks forward to the tangible proofs of
Your love, that will come again. In these hours of despair may
we admit our sinfulness and wretchedness, humbly know our
weakness and finally acknowledge that You alone are the true
source of all good and of all heavenly solace.

When You grant us Your comfort, let there come with it a
spirit of humility and of readiness to serve You even when we
are unconsoled.

Give us always a spirit of bravery and of bold resolve, to recognise temptation, not to dispute with it nor to compromise, but to give it an unequivocal refusal, for this is the simplest strategy. Give us the courage to ask advice in difficult situations, without false loquacity or self-admiration but also without that foolish pride which tells us we should always solve our own problems. Give us the spirit of heavenly wisdom, to see the real danger points of our characters and lives, to keep watch and to contend most constantly where we are most vulnerable.

In a word, Lord, give us Your Spirit. Grant us the fruits of the Spirit which according to the apostle are: charity, joy, peace, patience, benignity, goodness, faith, mildness, modesty, continence (Gal 5:22). If we have the Spirit and His fruits, then we are no longer slaves of the law but free children of God. The Spirit cries out in us: Abba, Father. He intercedes for us with unspeakable groanings. He is the anointing, the seal and the surety of eternal life. He is the fount of eternal water which has its source in the heart and rises up to eternal life, whispering: Come! Come home to the Father!

Jesus, send us the Spirit. Give us again and again Your Pentecostal gift. Make our spiritual eye bright and our spiritual awareness sensitive, so that we are able to distinguish Your Spirit from all others. Give us Your Spirit, that it may be said of us: "And if the Spirit of him who raised up Jesus from the dead dwell in You; he that raised up Jesus Christ from the dead shall quicken also your mortal bodies, because of his Spirit that dwelleth in you" (Rom 8:11).

Lord, may Pentecost be ever with us. Your servants and handmaids ask with the boldness which You require of them: May Pentecost be in us also. Now and for ever.

Amen.

# FREED BY GOD

God, Eternal Mystery of our Being, You have set us free because Your own infinity has become the limitless horizon of our life. You gathered us into safety by making everything but Your own infinitude provisional for us. You have made us present to Yourself by perpetually destroying all idols in us and around us. We want to worship them but they turn us to stone. It is because You alone are our infinite goal that we have an immense movement of hope ahead of us. If we truly and totally believed in You as the One Who gave Himself to us, we would be truly free. You promised us this victory since Jesus of Nazareth gained it in His death, for Himself and His brothers, by once more finding You as His Father even in the death of abandonment. In Him, Jesus of Nazareth, the Crucified and Risen One, we know for sure that neither ideas nor powers and dominions, neither the burden of tradition nor the utopian ideas of our futures, neither the gods of reason nor the gods of our own depths, nor really anything in or around us, can separate us from *that* love in which the unspeakable God in His all-embracing freedom has given Himself to us in Christ Jesus, our Lord.

Amen.

# GOD OF MY DAILY ROUTINE

I should like to bring the routine of my daily life before You, O Lord, to discuss the long days and tedious hours that are filled with everything else but You.

Look at this routine, O God of Mildness. Look upon us men, who are practically nothing else but routine. In Your loving mercy, look at my soul, a road crowded by a dense and endless column of bedraggled refugees, a bomb-pocked highway on which countless trivialities, much empty talk and pointless activity, idle curiosity and ludicrous pretensions of importance all roll forward in a never-ending stream.

When it stands before You and Your infallible Truthfulness, doesn't my soul look just like a marketplace where the second-hand dealers from all corners of the globe have assembled to sell the shabby riches of this world? Isn't it just like a noisy bazaar, where I and the rest of humanity display our cheap trinkets to the restless, milling crowds?

Many years ago, when I was a schoolboy distinguished by the name of "philosopher," I learned that the soul is somehow everything. O God, how the meaning of that lofty-sounding phrase has changed! How different it sounds to me now, when my soul has become a huge warehouse where day after day the trucks unload their crates without any plan or discrimination, to be piled helter-skelter in every available corner and cranny, until it is crammed full from top to bottom with the trite, the commonplace, the insignificant, the routine.

What will become of me, dear God, if my life goes on like this? What will happen to me when all the crates are suddenly swept out of the warehouse? How will I feel at the hour of my death? Then there will be no more "daily routine"; then I shall suddenly be abandoned by all the things that now fill up my days here on earth.

And what will I myself be at that hour, when I am only myself and nothing else? My whole life long I have been nothing but the ordinary routine, all business and activity, a desert filled with empty sound and meaningless fury. But when the heavy weight of death one day presses down upon my life and squeezes the true and lasting content out of all those many days and long years, what will be the final yield?

Maybe at that last reckoning, at the time of the great disillusionment that will take the place of the great illusion of my tritely spent earthly life, maybe then, O God, if You have been merciful to me, the genuine yield of my ungenuine life will be only a few blessed moments, made luminous and living by Your grace. Maybe then I shall see the few precious instants when the grace of Your love has succeeded in stealing into an obscure corner of my life, in between the countless bales of second-hand goods that fill up my everyday routine.

How can I redeem this wretched humdrum? How can I turn myself toward the one thing necessary, toward You? How can I escape from the prison of this routine? Haven't You Yourself committed me to it? And didn't I find myself already in exile, from the very first moment I began to realize that my true life must be directed toward You? Wasn't I already deeply entangled in the pettiness of everyday cares, when it first dawned on me that I must not allow myself to be suffocated under the weight of earthly routine?

Aren't You my Creator? Haven't You made me a human being? And what is man but a being that is not sufficient to itself, a being who sees his own insufficiency, so that he longs naturally and necessarily for Your Infinity? What is man but the being who must follow the urge to run toward Your distant stars, who must keep up his chase until he has covered all the highways and byways of this world, only in the end to see Your stars still coursing their serenely ordered way—and as far away as ever?

Even if I should try to escape from my routine by becoming a Carthusian, so that I'd have nothing more to do but spend my days in silent adoration of Your holy presence, would that solve my problem? Would that really lift me out of my rut?

I'm afraid not, since not even the sacred actions I now perform are free from the corrosive dust of this spirit of routine. When I think of all the hours I have spent at Your holy altar, or reciting Your Church's official prayer in my Breviary, then it becomes clear to me that I myself am responsible for making my life so humdrum. It's not the affairs of the world that make my days dull and insignificant; I myself have dug the rut. Through my own attitude I can transform the holiest events into the grey tedium of dull routine. My days don't make *me* dull—it's the other way around.

That's why I now see clearly that, if there is any path at all on which I can approach You, it must lead through the very middle of my ordinary daily life. If I should try to flee to You by any other way, I'd actually be leaving myself behind, and that, aside from being quite impossible, would accomplish nothing at all.

But is there a path through my daily life that leads to You? Doesn't this road take me ever farther away from You? Doesn't it immerse me all the more deeply in the empty noise of worldly activity, where You, God of Quiet, do not dwell?

I realize that we gradually get tired of the feverish activity that seems so important to a young mind and heart. I know that the *taedium vitae*, of which the moral philosophers speak, and the feeling of satiety with life, which Your Scripture reports as the final earthly experience of Your patriarchs, will also become more and more my own lot. My daily routine will automatically turn into the great melancholy of life, thus indirectly leading me to You, the infinite counterpart of this earthly emptiness.

But I don't have to be a Christian to know that—don't the pagans experience it too? Is this the way my everyday life is supposed to lead to You? Do I come into Your presence just because this life has revealed its true face to me, finally admitting that all is vanity, all is misery?

Isn't that the road to despair rather than the way to You? Isn't it the crowning victory for routine, when a man's burned-out heart no longer finds the least bit of joy in things that formerly gave him relief, when even the simple things of his ordinary life, which he used to be able to call upon to help him over the periods of boredom and emptiness, have now become tasteless to him?

Is a tired and disillusioned heart any closer to You than a young and happy one? Where can we ever hope to find You, if neither our simple joys nor ordinary sorrows succeed in revealing You to us? Indeed our day-to-day pleasures seem somehow especially designed to make us forget about You, and with our daily disappointments it's no better: they make our hearts so sick and bitter that we seem to lose any talent we ever had for discovering You.

O God, it seems we can lose sight of You in anything we do. Not even prayer, or the Holy Sacrifice, or the quiet of the cloister, not even the great disillusion with life itself can fully safeguard us from this danger. And thus it's clear that even these sacred, non-routine things belong ultimately to our routine. It's evident that routine is not just a part of my life, not even just the greatest part, but the whole. *Every* day is "everyday." Everything I do is routine, because everything can rob me of the one and only thing I really need, which is You, my God.

But on the other hand, if it's true that I can lose You in everything, it must also be true that I can find You in everything. If You have given me no single place to which I can flee and be sure of finding You, if anything I do can mean the loss of You, than I must be able to find You in every place, in each and every thing I do. Otherwise I couldn't find You at all, and this cannot be, since I can't possibly exist without You. Thus I must seek You in all things. If every day is "everyday," then every day is *Your* day, and every hour is the hour of Your grace.

Everything is "everyday" and Your day together. And thus, my God, I again understand something I have always known. A truth has again come to life in my heart, which my reason has already often told me—and of what value is a truth of reason when it is not also the life of the heart?

Again and again I must take out the old notebook in which I copied that short but vital passage from Ruysbroeck many years ago. I must reread it, so that my heart can regrasp it. I always find consolation in rediscovering how this truly pious man felt about his own life. And the fact that I still love these words after so many years of routine living is to me a sacred pledge that You will one day bless *my* ordinary actions too.

God comes to us continually, both directly and indirectly. He demands of us both work and pleasure, and wills that each should not be hindered, but rather strengthened, by the other. Thus the interior man possesses his life in both these ways, in activity and in rest. And he is whole and undivided in each of them, for he is entirely in God when he joyfully rests, and he is entirely in himself when he actively loves.

The interior man is constantly being challenged and admonished by God to renew both his rest and his work. Thus he finds justice; thus he makes his way to God with sincere love and everlasting works. He enters into God by means of the pleasure-giving tendency to eternal rest. And while he abides in God, still he goes out to all creatures in an all-embracing love, in virtue and justice. And that is the highest stage of the interior life.

Those who do not possess both rest and work in one and
the same exercise, have not yet attained this kind of justice.
No just man can be hindered in his interior recollection, for
he recollects himself as much in pleasure as in activity. He
is like a double mirror, reflecting images on both sides. In the
higher part of his spirit he receives God together with all His
gifts; in the lower he takes in corporeal images through his
senses. . . .

I must learn to have both "everyday" and Your day in the
same exercise. In devoting myself to the works of the world, I
must learn to give myself to You, to possess You, the One and
Only Thing, in everything. But how? Only through You, O
God. Only through Your help can I be an "interior" man in the
midst of my many and varied daily tasks. Only through You
can I continue to be in myself with You, when I go out of
myself to be with the things of the world.

It's not anxiety or non-being, not even death that can rescue
me from being lost to the things of the world. Not the modern
philosophers, but only Your love can save me, the love of You,
who are the goal and attraction of all things. Only You are
fulfillment and satiety, You who are sufficient even unto
Yourself. It is only the love of You, my Infinite God, which
pierces the very heart of all things, at the same time transcend-
ing them all and leaping upward into the endless reaches of
Your Being, catching up all the lost things of earth and trans-
forming them into a hymn of praise to Your Infinity.

Before You, all multiplicity becomes one; in You, all that has
been scattered is reunited; in Your Love all that has been
merely external is made again true and genuine. In Your Love
all the diffusion of the day's chores comes home again to the
evening of Your unity, which is eternal life.

This love, which can allow my daily routine to remain
routine and still transform it into a home-coming to You, this
love only You can give. So what should I say to You now, as

I come to lay my everyday routine before You? There is only one thing I can beg for, and that is Your most ordinary and most exalted gift, the grace of Your Love.

Touch my heart with this grace, O Lord. When I reach out in joy or in sorrow for the things of this world, grant that through them I may know and love You, their Maker and final home. You who are Love itself, give me the grace of love, give me Yourself, so that all my days may finally empty into the one day of Your eternal Life.

# THE LIFE OF GRACE

Lord Jesus Christ, we worship You through our faith in Your death, which is our redemption. But when our spirit feels its way toward You, then through Your Spirit we are in You and You in us. For You laid Your hand upon us when we were baptized. You have poured out Your Spirit into our hearts. You accepted our sinfulness and overcame it with Your grace. You enlarged the scope of our human nature into the incomprehensible infinities of Your Father. We have become greater than we can ever imagine or understand. We are more than our everyday life or even the highest and deepest of our experiences can reveal, as long as we wander in the darkness of this world. We are anointed with Your Spirit, sanctified through Your grace, born again to the life of God's true children, participating in the divine nature, sealed unto eternal life. Your remoteness, the remoteness of the eternal God, the remoteness of his blinding truth and his austere sanctity, his burning love and his boundless flowing life, has become nearness. It has become part of us. For we have Your Holy Spirit. He is the anointing oil and the eternal seal of our innermost being. He is the fulfillment of all the bottomless depths of our existence. He is the life in us through which we have already overcome death. He is the unbounded happiness, which has dried up the very last streams of our tears, even when their floodwaters had risen over all the lowlands of our experience. He is God dwelling in us, the holiness of our heart, its secret rejoicing, its strength, which is always wonderfully there, even when our own strength fails and we are at our wits' end. He is in us, giving us faith and inward knowledge, although we are blind fools. For he is all-knowing and he is ours. He is the hope in us, which does not founder in any of the shipwrecks of our own despair. He is the love in us, which loves us and which makes us love, generously, exultantly in spite of our cold, small and narrow hearts. He is eternal youth in us, in the despair-filled senility of our time and of our hearts. He is the laughter which sounds softly behind our tears. He is the confidence which bears us up, the freedom, the winged happiness of our souls. We are greater than we know. In acknowledging this, we do You honor, Lord, we contradict ourselves and our experience of ourselves for Your Word's sake. Even if we have really learned what we are, hollow and empty, bottomless and wretched, this knowledge of our finiteness and sinfulness is still a part of that sinfulness and tells us nothing real about ourselves. For this reason we believe Your word. What it tells us about ourselves is complete reality, *the* reality. It is the truth and the love of God—still hidden yet present, a matter of faith and yet a certain possession, the torment of our hope and the goad of unending restlessness, yet the confidence and comfort of eternal life too; the strength of the constant movement of time yet the peace of the eternal

Sabbath; the judgment of our sins yet also the word which absolves us from them.

We kneel, O Lord, before Your Sacrament, as Your people. Before the Sacrament of Your death, which gives us life; before the Sacrament of Your silence, which speaks out more clearly than all the chatter of our own hearts; before the Sacrament of Your Body, which, ascended from this earth, is the guarantee of heaven. Gazing up at that body we implore You: Live in us and let Your Spirit fill us. We believe in Your strength, which conquers through our weakness, in Your mercy which has already triumphed over our wretchedness, in Your truth which has overcome our lies, in Your freedom which has enlarged our narrowness. Live in us. Let us obey Your commandments joyfully in Your spirit, which no longer needs any law. Let us hope bravely against all hope even for the blessings of this earth. For Your spirit can change even the face of the earth. Not heaven alone, but the earth too shall be full of Your glory. Even if we are defeated in the struggle for this new world, we shall bear the palm of life, so long as we have fought bravely for it to the end. We do not know whom Your grace has already blessed and transformed, among all those who seem to be far from You; we feel ourselves no better than those who think they are still groping in the darkness, than those whose deeds, and therefore whose hearts, outwardly at least contradict Your commandments. It is, then, not our word but Yours which is the last we can or will say of ourselves, the word of your grace. The Spirit in which we affirm our faith is Your Holy Spirit. We are pardoned now and, with Your grace, for all eternity.

Amen.

# PRAYER FOR HOPE

We ask You, God of grace and eternal life, to increase and strengthen hope in us. Give us this virtue of the strong, this power of the confident, this courage of the unshakable. Make us always have a longing for You, the infinite plenitude of being. Make us always build on You and Your fidelity, always hold fast without despondency to Your might. Make us to be of this mind and produce this attitude in us by Your Holy Spirit. Then, our Lord and God, we shall have the virtue of hope. Then we can courageously set about the task of our life again and again. Then we shall be animated by the joyful confidence that we are not working in vain. Then we shall do our work in the knowledge that in us and through us and, where our powers fail, without us, You the almighty according to Your good pleasure are working to Your honor and our salvation. Strengthen Your hope in us.

The hope of eternity, however, Eternal God, is Your only begotten Son. He possesses Your infinite nature from eternity to eternity, because You have communicated it to him and ever communicate it, in eternal generation. He therefore possesses all that we hope and desire. He is wisdom and power, beauty and goodness, life and glory, he is all in all. And he, this Son to whom You have given all, has become ours. He became man. Your eternal Word, God of Glory, became man, became like one of us, humbled himself and took human form, a human body, a human soul, a human life, a human lot even in its most terrible possibilities. Your Son, Heavenly Father, truly became man. We kneel in adoration. For who can measure this incomprehensible love of Yours? You have loved the world so much that men take offense at Your love and call the affirmation of the incarnation of Your Son folly and madness. But we believe in the incomprehensibility, the overwhelming audacity of Your love. And because we believe, we can exult in blessed hope: Christ in us is the hope of glory. For if You give us Your Son, what can there be You have held back, what can there be which You have refused us? If we possess Your Son to whom You have given everything, Your own substance, what could still be lacking to us? And he is truly ours. For he is the Son of Mary, who is our sister in Adam, he is a child of Adam's family, of the same race as we are, one in substance and origin with man. And if we human beings in Your plans and according to Your will as creator are all to form a great community of descent and destiny, and if Your Son is to belong to this one great community, then we, precisely we poor children of Eve, share the race and lot of Your own Son. We are brothers of the only-begotten, the brethren of Your Son, co-heirs of his glory. We share in his grace, in his Spirit, in his life, in his destiny through Cross and glorification, in his eternal glory. It is no longer *we* who live our life but Christ our brother lives his life in us and through us. We are ready, Father of Jesus Christ and our Father, to share in the life of Your Son. Dispose of our life, make it conformable to the life of Your Son. He wills to continue his own life in us until the end of time, he wills to reveal in us and in our life the glory, the greatness, beauty and the blessed power of his life. What meets us in life is not chance, is not blind fate but is a part of the life of Your Son. The joy we shall receive as Christ's joy, success as his success, pain as his pain, sorrow as his sorrow, work as his work, death as a sharing of his death.

In one respect we ask especially for Your grace. Make us share in Jesus' prayer. He is the great worshiper of God in spirit and in truth, he is the mediator through whom alone our prayer can reach to the throne of grace. We wish to pray in him, united with his prayer. May he, with whom we are united in his Spirit, teach us to pray. May he teach us to pray as he himself prayed, to pray at all times and not to slacken, to pray perseveringly, confidently, humbly, in spirit and in truth, with true love of our neighbor without which no prayer is pleasing to You. May he teach us to pray for what he prayed: that Your name may be hallowed, Your will be done, Your Kingdom come to us, for only if we first pray in that way for Your honor will You also hear us if we pray for ourselves, our earthly well-being and earthly cares. Give us the spirit of prayer, of recollection, of union with God. Lord, accept my poor heart. It is often so far from You. It is like a waste land without water, lost in the innumerable things and trifles that fill my everday life. Only You, Lord, can focus my heart on You, who are the center of all hearts and the Lord of every soul. Only You can give the spirit of prayer, only Your grace is capable of granting me to find You through the multiplicity of things and the distraction of mind of everyday routine, You the one thing necessary, the one thing in which my heart can rest. May Your Spirit come to the help of my weakness, and when we do not know what we should ask, may he intercede for us with inexpressible sighs. and You who know men's hearts will hear what Your Spirit interceding for us desires in us.

Finally, however, I ask You for the hardest and most difficult, for the grace to recognize the Cross of Your Son in all the suffering of my life, to adore Your holy and inscrutable will in it, to follow Your Son on his way to the Cross as long as it may please You. Make me sensitive in what concerns Your honor and not merely for my own well-being, and then I also will be able to carry many a cross as atonement for my sins. Do not let me be embittered by suffering but mature, patient, selfless, gentle and filled with longing for that land where there is no pain and for that day when You will wipe all tears from the eyes of those who have loved You and in sorrow have believed in Your love and in darkness have believed in Your light. Let my pain be a profession of my faith in Your promises, a profession of my hope in Your goodness and fidelity, a profession of my love, that I love You more than myself, that I love You for Your own sake even without reward. May the Cross of my Lord be my model, my power, my consolation, the solution of all obscure questions, the light of every darkness. Grant that we may glory in the Cross of our Lord Jesus Christ, grant us to become so mature in true Christian being and life that we no longer regard the cross as a misfortune and incomprehensible meaninglessness but as a sign of Your election, as the secret, sure sign that we are Yours for ever. For it is a faithful saying that if we die with him we shall also live with him and if we endure with him, we shall also reign with him. Father, we will to share everything with Your Son, his life, his divine glory, and therefore his suffering and his death. Only with the cross, give the strength to bear it. Cause us to experience in the cross its blessing also. Give us the cross which Your wisdom knows is for our salvation and not our ruin.

Son of the Father, Christ who lives in us, You are our hope of glory. Live in us, bring our life under the laws of Your life, make our life like to Yours. Live in me, pray in me, suffer in me, more I do not ask. For if I have You I am rich; those who find You have found the power and the victory of their life.

Amen.

# GOD OF MY VOCATION

O God my Father, You are the God of free favors, of grace freely given. You show Your mercy to whomever You please, where and when You choose.

If it's true that Your calling of human beings to a share in Your own Life is a completely free gift, then, as I well understand, this summons is not something given to every man along with his nature. Man finds You only where You choose to be found.

And as proof that Your salvation is a gratuitous gift, every man's road to eternal life, even though it leads to Your Infinity which is everywhere, must still take the "detour" through that definite human being who was born in Palestine under Emperor Augustus and died under the Governor, Pontius Pilate. We must take the "indirect route" leading through Your Son Who became man. Your grace comes to us not in the "always and everywhere" of Your all-pervasive Spirit, but in the "here and now" of Jesus Christ.

Your Holy Spirit blows where He will—where *He* will, not where I will. He is not simply always there, whenever and wherever a man wants Him to be. We must go to Him, there where He chooses to give His grace. And that's why Your salvation is bound up with Your visible Church. That's why Your grace comes to us in visible signs.

This is all quite clear to me, Lord, and I'm very happy about this distinctive characteristic of Your grace. It's comforting to know that I can approach You not merely in the realm of "pure spirit"—this "pure spirit" about which the philosophers talk, when they start founding religions, has always struck me as being not spirit, but a pure ghost, anyway—but in concrete, tangible, visible signs. It warms my heart to know that I can be sure of Your power and presence in my life through the water of baptism, or by the audible word of forgiveness spoken by the priest, or in the holy bread of the altar.

For my part I want no religion of pure spirit, of pure internal experience. Basically, such a religion is a mere human invention, in which man ends up grasping only himself, instead of You. He plumbs only the shallow waters of his own spirit, and penetrates only his own poverty-stricken interior, instead of sounding the depths opened up by Your free word. And Your word tells us more of You than You could ever write in the narrow pages of Your creation.

But, my God, this arrangement of combined internal and external worship has brought something into my life which often lies heavily on my soul. You have made me Your priest, and have thus chosen me to be an earthly sign of Your grace to others. You have put Your grace into my hands, Your truth into my mouth. And although it doesn't surprise me that men should recognize You when You come to meet them in Your only-begotten Son, or in the chaste water of baptism, or in the silent form of the host, or in the words of Scripture so simple and yet so profound, still I find it all but incredible that You desire to come into Your Kingdom in the hearts of men through *me*. How can people possibly recognize You in *me?*

Indeed You have gone so far as to give me, along with my priesthood, also all the other means You use to convey Your loving greeting to men. You have equipped me with Your word, Your truth, Your sacraments. And You have attached these things to my ministry in such a way that they penetrate into the inmost regions of free souls only when these souls accept *me,* only when they take *me* along in the bargain.

Can people really recognize You in me? Or can they at least

grasp the fact that You have sent me as the ambassador of Your truth, the bearer of Your mercy? When this question occurs to me, it seems that Your Gospel of joy for my brethren is to me, the messenger, only a crushing burden.

I realize that You have sent me, that I am Your messenger—maybe a very pitiful one, but for all that still Your messenger, a man sent by You and stamped with Your ineffaceable seal. Your truth does not become false just because *I* preach it, even though I too am a sinful man, to whom the dictum can be applied: *omnis homo mendax*, "every man is a liar."

Your grace remains pure, even when it is dispensed through *my* hands. Your Gospel is still the good tidings of great joy, even when it's not particularly noticeable that *my* soul is exulting in God my Savior. And Your light continues to shine forth, changing the dark death-shadows of our earth into the brilliant noonday of Your grace, even when this light has to find its way to human beings through the cracked and dusty panes of *my* tiny lantern.

I know, Lord, that as a priest of Your true Church, I should not let the sense of my vocation, and the courage to preach Your Gospel in season and out of season, depend on the consciousness of my own personal worth. Your priest does not approach people as a revivalist or an enthusiast, not as a purveyor of mystic wisdom or gnostic or pentecostal prophet, or whatever else such persons may call themselves. These can communicate to others no more of You than they have themselves. But as a priest, I come as Your legate, as a messenger sent by Your Son, our Lord. And that is at the same time less and more, a thousand times more than anything else.

But, O God of my calling, it would be so much easier if I could just deliver Your message and then, when Your work is done, go back to living my own life. Then the burden of being Your messenger would be no heavier than that of any other messenger or administrator who does his job and is done with it. But Your charge to me, Your commission itself has become my very life. It ruthlessly claims all my energies for itself; it lives from my own life.

As Your messenger, I can live my own personal life only by passing on Your word. I am Your messenger and nothing more. Your lamp—excuse me for being so bold, Lord—burns with the oil of my life. In Your service there are no office hours after which a man can close up shop and be his own master again. I can never forget that I am Your servant and go back to being a mere "private citizen."

Truly it's an unspeakable honor and privilege to be able to serve You with all one's energy. I must thank You that You have turned my life to Your service, that I have no other "profession" than conveying the message of Your salvation. I must be eternally grateful that, in my life, profession and devotion are completely identical—there is no distinction between what I do out of duty and what I do out of love.

And yet, if it were only possible in Your service, as in every other, to separate official business from one's private life! How much easier it would be! And I don't say this because I would prefer to give You only a few hours' service a day, and spend more time communicating to others my own religious experiences and inspirations, setting them on fire with my own enthusiasm and conviction. On the contrary, I want to be *Your* messenger, the transmitter of *Your* truth and *Your* grace, and nothing more. And precisely because that's what I want, I sometimes wish that people could better distinguish my official position from my private life.

Can one pass on Your truth without having fully grasped it himself? Can I preach Your Gospel, if it has not struck deep roots in my own heart? Can I pass on Your Life, if I am not alive with it myself? Your holy signs can produce grace of their own power, it's true. But would my fellow men allow *me* to mark them with these signs, unless my own countenance were to them a sign that You had sent me? It's unavoidable: Your official business and my private life cannot be separated.

And that is precisely the burden of my life. For look, Lord: even when I announce Your pure truth, I'm still preaching my own narrowness and mediocrity along with it. I'm still presenting myself, the "average man." How can I bring my hearers to distinguish between You and me in the frightful mixture of You and me that I call my sermons? How can I teach them to take Your word to their hearts, and forget me, the preacher?

I want to be a transmitter of Your light, and to do so, I must nourish it with the oil of my life. And yet I can't avoid placing myself before the lantern, coming between Your light and the searching eyes of my fellow men. I seem to be good for nothing at all but making the already-dark shadows of this world even darker and longer.

I understand all too well that, at the end of my priestly life, I shall have been only Your poor, unprofitable servant. I shall have been the messenger whom You have sent on ahead, who, instead of clearing the way for You, more often succeeds only in being a roadblock. Any grace that goes out from me is *Your* grace. Whatever of mine goes out from me is nothing, only a hindrance or, at best, a means You employ to test my fellow men, to see whether their instinctive love can recognize You, even when You disguise Yourself, almost beyond all recognition, by appearing to them in me.

O God of my vocation, when I consider these things, I must confess that I don't at all feel like taking my place in the proud ranks of Your confident and conquering apostles. I rather feel that I should be on my way, simply and humbly, walking in fear and trembling. I don't mean to criticize those among my brethren who can be so happily sure of themselves, those of

Your servants who so unmistakably reflect the inner confidence that they are coming in the name of the Lord God of Hosts, and who are quite amazed if anyone does not immediately recognize in them the ambassadors of the Almighty.

I cannot belong to that fortunate group, O Lord. Grant me rather the grace to belong to the number of Your lowly servants who are rather amazed when they are received by their fellow human beings. Let my heart tremble again and again in grateful surprise at the miracles of Your grace, which is mighty in the midst of weakness. Let me continue to marvel that I meet so many persons who allow me, poor sinner that I am, to enter into the secret chamber of their hearts, because they have been able to recognize You hidden in me.

Thus I shall be happy to set out again and again on my messenger's rounds to my fellow human beings. You have sent me, and so I go in Your name, not my own. Let Your power triumph through my weakness, whenever You desire it to do so.

As I proceed with Your message along the pathway of my life, I shall no doubt often experience what befell Your prophet of long ago: I shall be disillusioned with Jahweh, laughed to scorn by people, a man of contention before the whole world. Then I must speak out—and woe is me, if I do not—I must speak of You, the One whom it is more fitting to honor by silence. I must speak, even with the tormenting feeling of being mere sounding brass and tinkling cymbal. For who can really know for certain whether or not he possesses the love without which everything else is just hollow noise?

In the strength of Your word I shall march continually around the Jericho of human souls, even with their laughter ringing in my ears, until You bring its walls crashing down. You will do this of Your own power, so that no one can boast before You of his prowess over souls. Thus will my mission be fulfilled, in the same way as was that of Your Son, my crucified Master. And for this, may You be praised for all eternity.

O God of my vocation, I am only a poor mask, behind which You have chosen to approach human beings as the hidden God. Grant me the grace day by day to be ever more free from sin and self-seeking. Even then I shall remain what I can't help being, Your disguise and Your unprofitable servant. But then at least I shall grow ever more like Your Son, Who also had to envelop the eternal light of His divinity in the form of a servant, to be found in the garb and livery of a man.

When I bear the burden of Your calling, when Your mission weighs down heavily upon me, when Your Majesty humbles me, and my weakness is taken up into that of Your Son, then I may confidently trust that the hindrance which I have been to Your coming may still turn out to be a blessing to my brothers. Then perhaps You will transubstantiate my servitude—for only You could work such a change, unseen by me and my fellow human beings—into a somehow sacramental form, under whose poverty You will be the bread of life for my brethren.

O God of my vocation, let my life be consumed as the Sacred Host, so that my brothers and I may live in You, and You in us, for all eternity.

# GOD OF MY BROTHERS

You have sent me to work among men, O God. You have laid the heavy burden of Your authority and Your sacred powers upon my shoulders, and bid me go out to Your creatures, whom You want to save. In a strict, almost brusque command, You have sent me away from Yourself, ordered me out among men.

Of course I had already spent most of my time associating with men anyway, even before Your word of consecration sent me out. I used to love it, to love and be loved, to be a close friend and to have close friends. It's an easy and very pleasant thing to be among men in this way. You visit only those You Yourself have chosen, and stay as long as You please.

But now things are different. The men to whom I have been sent are of Your choosing, Lord, not mine. And I must be not their friend, but their servant. And when I get tired of them, it's not a sign that I should get up and leave, as it used to be, but rather a sign of Your command to stay.

O God, what strange creatures these men are, for whose sake You have chased me away from You! For the most part they won't even listen to me when I come in Your name. They have absolutely no desire for Your grace and Your truth, the gifts You have given me to bring to them. And yet I must keep pounding on their doors again and again, like an unwanted but persistent peddler.

If I only knew that they were really rejecting You when they refuse to admit me, that would be some consolation. At least I wouldn't have to reproach myself for doing my job so badly. But as it is, I can't get rid of the agonizing thought that maybe even I would refuse to open the door, if someone came and knocked on it the way I do, claiming to be sent by You.

And even those who let me in don't treat me much better. They usually want everything but what I'm trying to bring. They want to tell me their little cares and worries; they want to pour out their hearts to me. And what a conglomeration comes spilling out! What a disheartening mixture of the comical and the tragic, of small truth and big lies, of little trials that are taken too seriously and big sins that are made light of!

And what do these men want of me? Sometimes it's material help, sometimes just the consolation of a sympathetic heart. Or if it's not that, then they look upon me as some kind of celestial insurance agent, with whom they can take out an accident policy for eternity, to make sure that You never break in upon their lives with the Omnipotence of Your Holiness and Justice. They want to sign a contract preventing You from ever shaking them out of their petty little weekday concerns and Sunday amusements, to bind You to an agreement whereby You'll leave them in peace, both in this life and in the next.

How seldom does anyone say, "Lord, what do You want me to do?" How rare it is that anyone really wants to hear the whole, unadulterated, and astounding message that we must love *You* passionately, and not ourselves, for *Your* sake, and not our own, and that we must *love* You, not just respect You and fear Your judgment. How seldom anyone wants to receive a gift of Your grace the way it really is: austere and plain, for Your honor, not just for our consolation, chaste and pure, silent and bold.

These are the men to whom You have sent me, and I cannot escape them. For their defects are not a signal to me to flee out of the land of the all-too-human, but rather a sign that I have really found the field in which You, O mysterious and extravagant God, want me to sow the seed of Your grace and Your truth, even with all its rocks and thorns and hard-trodden paths.

I must sow the seed and then watch how it falls by the wayside, upon the rocks, among thorns, how it is eaten by the birds of the air, all unfruitful. And even where it seems to fall upon good earth, it no sooner begins to spring up than it takes on the characteristics of the earth in which it took root, and thus is doomed to be blighted by petty human failings. The true fruit that it brings—thirty, sixty and a hundred-fold—only You seem to be able to see that. When I think I see it, I must still doubt, for haven't You Yourself said that none of us knows who is really worthy of Your Kingdom?

When I complain this way to You, about my brethren to whom You have sent me, I don't mean to say that I am any better than they. I know my own heart, and You know it still better. It's no different from the hearts of the men I must approach in Your name.

When I complain to You of the heavy burden of my vocation, I know that I am acting exactly like those about whom I have just been complaining. I am acting like a small man who wants to be consoled, who is always thinking of his own sorrows, who can't for a minute forget his own troubles and his own comfort to lose himself in silent admiration of what a great thing it is to spend one's life in unselfishly serving You.

And that's just why it all looks so hopeless: haven't I enough burdens of my own to bear? Isn't my heart weak and miserable enough with its own troubles, without adding to it the crushing woes of others?

Or is that the very way my heart is meant to grow strong, by devoting itself patiently and uncomplainingly to the bearing of others' burdens? Do I regain my own inner strength precisely by being steadfast and courageous in the service of my brethren, and thereby giving testimony to the world that Your Heart is bigger than ours, that You are patient and long-suffering, that Your Mercy never disdains us, that Your Love is never outdone by our wretchedness? Is that the best way to take care of myself, by forgetting myself in the care of others?

If Your sending me out was an act of Your Mercy to me, O Lord—and how can I doubt that it was?—then it must be so. Then You must desire that I possess my own soul in patience, precisely through bearing in patience the souls of my brethren.

But look, my God, when I approach men with Your truth and Your grace—almost as if I were bringing them the last sacraments—when I knock on the door of their interior life and they let me in, they usually lead me only into the rooms in which they live their ordinary daily lives.

They tell me about themselves and their worldly affairs; they show me their poor earthly furniture. They talk a lot about trivialities, in order to stay away from the one subject that's really important. They try to make themselves and me forget why I have actually come, to bring You like the Blessed Sacrament into the inmost chamber of their hearts, where the eternal spark in them is sick unto death, where an altar to You should be erected, on which the candles of faith, hope, and love should be burning.

Instead of this, they receive me into the dingy rooms of their ordinary surface-life. These doors I have absolutely no trouble in opening. But I seek in vain for an entrance into the last depths where a man's eternal destiny is decided. In fact, it often seems to me that these men themselves have never found the door to that inner sanctuary where every man is sick unto death—or unto life. How then should I be able to find it?

Maybe it's all part of Your plan, that I never succeed in penetrating this door. Perhaps I am meant to be only an errand-boy who leaves Your gift and Your message at the delivery entrance, with no thought of being invited inside. Maybe it's just not my business to enter the interior castle of another's soul, to try to make sure that Your message and Your gift really become this man's eternal life through his freely given love.

Is that how it is? Do You want to be completely alone with the soul in this single decisive moment? Do You prefer to act alone in the center of a man's heart when he performs this all-important act? Is my task finished when I have "done my duty" and delivered my message? Can't I, or shouldn't I even try to carry You into the last depths of my fellow man, because You are already present there, just as You fill every part of whatever lives or exists, and are already present in every man to his eternal judgment or salvation?

But if You have commanded me really to care for souls, and not just to take care of my own "duty," then I must be able to penetrate into that hidden inner chamber. I must have some way of reaching the very center of their being, of touching the very tip of their soul. And if it's true that You alone have really found the way there, You with Your grace, against whose gentle omnipotence no heart succeeds in sealing itself off when You will to exercise Your mercy, then I am sure that You alone are the way I must go and the door through which I must pass, in order to find the soul of my brother.

I must find my way to You and penetrate ever more deeply into You, if I am not to be simply a more or less welcome guest, whom my fellow men put up with in the course of their daily routine. Only thus can I enter that last redoubt which is the abode of Your eternal light, or of eternal darkness.

No matter how hard men try to break off relations with You, You are always present to them. Even when they attempt to lock and bolt their souls against You, You are there at the very core of these futile efforts. You are present in Your unfathomable Love and Omnipotence, which hold sway even over the kingdom of evey man's freedom. And thus it is that one who is entrusted with the help and care of souls can draw near to them only by drawing near to You, O King of All Hearts.

So You haven't really sent me away from You, after all. When You assigned me the task of going out among men, You were only repeating to me Your one and only commandment: to find my way home to You in love. All care of souls is ultimately possible only in union with You, only in the love which binds me to You and thus makes me Your companion in finding a path to the hearts of men.

You are waiting to be found in love, and that which is the heart and soul of true love of You, prayer. If I had prayed more, I would be closer to souls. For prayer, when it is not just a begging for Your favors, enables me to grow in intimate, loving union with You. Thus it is not merely a useful aid in my work for souls, but the very first and last act of my apostolate.

Lord, teach me to pray and to love You. Then I shall forget my own wretchedness on account of You, for I shall be able to do the one thing that lets me forget it: patiently bear the poverty of my brethren into the land of Your riches. Then, united with You, O God of my Brothers, I shall really be able to be a brother to them. I shall be able to help them in the one thing that is really necessary: finding You.

# PRAYER FOR THE CHURCH

I shall pray for the Church, my God, each day during the celebration of the Eucharist. My faith can only survive in the community of those who together form the holy Church of Jesus Christ. And therefore (among other reasons) it is essential to my own salvation that she be the very home and foundation of my faith.

I know of course that she always is and always will be this for me through the power of Your tender mercy. Yet because she is also the Church of poor sinners she can only serve as a foundation and a dwelling place to an entirely different extent:

she can make it easier or more difficult for me to believe in You and in Your victorious love for me. Truthfully though, I do not consider myself to be any better than others in the Church; I know that I am anything but a sterling argument for the origin of the Church in the mercy of God's will—I who am a member of this Church and am supposed to represent it.

But I should therefore wish to add that my sisters and brothers in this Church will just as vehemently take issue with me should I pray: I believe in one holy, catholic and apostolic Church, the communion of saints, and the life everlasting. How tiresome, feeble-minded, short-sighted, and tyrannical "office holders" in the Church appear to me to be at times, solely concerned with the reputation of the organization and, in the worst sense, conservative and clerical. And when they unctiously and irritatingly display their noble intentions and their selflessness, it becomes even more annoying because I only too rarely hear them publicly and audibly confess their errors and mistaken judgments, but instead ask that we today believe in their infallibility and forget what major blunders and transgressions they committed the day before. How often are they morally outraged about a certain incident—their righteous anger about some social arrangement or other, the reason for which I see less clearly. They do a great deal of moralizing, yet far less is heard of the ecstatic joy, bursting hearts and minds, prompted by the message of Your grace in which You bestow Your very self. And indeed, would that greater perspective were included in their trite homilies; would that they made so much as a passing reference in praise of Your magnificent grace, the abundance of life, which You impart to us.

It is certainly not my intention to speak of the official conduct within Your Church, which often appears to me so limited in horizons, as if the Church was not a universal Church but rather a European one, peddling its wares to the rest of humanity. Three hundred years ago we burned witches, and a sorry thing it would have been had one ever doubted that witches did exist. Today this wholesale madness no longer exists, yet do we know for certain that other forms of madness are not still afoot among those who naively conform in the Church? Among those partisan supporters of the old madness may be included saintly, learned, and pious folk of good intention who failed to see how their actions contradicted the Gospel of Jesus Christ. Is the Church of today immune to the atrocities which occurred in former times? How do I come to know this? How then is one to find proof of such immunity?

God, have mercy upon us poor, short-sighted, and foolish sinners, we who form the body of Your Church. Have mercy upon those who call themselves Your representatives (in all honesty, I find that word inadequate because God simply cannot be represented). Have mercy upon us. I do not wish to belong in the company of those who find fault with the officials of the Church and yet bear more responsibility than they for the fact that Your Church appears to lack credibility. I desire even less to belong in the company of those who naively consider whether or not they are still willing to remain in the Church. I shall continue to labor on behalf of the far-sighted among us who are able to glimpse the miracles of Your divine Grace occurring within the Church itself. I must confess that I see these miracles more plainly among the young people in the Church (Andrea, for instance, who worked for an entire year without pay as a laundress in a home for abandoned youths during the course of her studies) than among the adults whose comfortable, middle-class existence goes its inevitable way. But perhaps my weary eyes do not allow me to view "authority" and "power" without becoming unduly emotional.

One may, in all good conscience, sing praises to the sanctity of the Church. It professes for all times Your divine grace and

Your unspeakable grandeur above and beyond anything which can be imagined. Therefore it shall endure until the end of time, even though I await the Kingdom of God, which will also bring an end to the Church. But even a somewhat bitter lament and a plea for divine mercy toward the Church still praise this Church and Your mercy.

# PRAYER ON THE EVE OF ORDINATION

Tomorrow, my God, I shall hear the words: *postulat sancta mater ecclesia, ut hos praesentes diaconos ad onus presbyterii ordinetis.*

So Your Church wills it. You in Your Church. I have not chosen You, You have chosen me. Blessed choice, since it is Your choice, the choice of Your unfathomable ways which are love and compassion.

Terrifying choice, made by You who choose in the perfect freedom and serenity of Your sovereign governance, who choose weak men to make them superhuman, those that are the least to make them the greatest, so that none may boast, so that God's power may be perfect only in our weakness. O make me understand that Your word "my yoke is sweet and my burden is light" holds good of the *onus presbyterii* too, so that the crushing burden of the cross of Your priesthood may become for me God's blessed burden, weighing me down with every grace. And then I shall hear the bishop ask: *scisne illos esse dignos?* Who is worthy of You, my God? Who is worthy before You? Nothingness before Your sovereign being, sinfulness before Your all-consuming sanctity. Lo, I must pray as

Isaiah did when he was called to be a prophet and heard the Sanctus of the adoring seraph: "Woe is me! For I am lost; for I am a man of unclean lips."

But You make me worthy, because Your call, Your grace and strength, are my worthiness; and since Isaiah, despite my *Domine non sum dignus*, I may boldly and confidently say *Adsum*—Here am I! Send me.

And then the bishop will silently lay his hands on my head, and in this silence, as on a Christmas Eve or Easter Eve— *dum silentium tenet omnia*—Your almighty Word and the fire of Your Spirit will make me into a priest of Your Son my Lord. Your Spirit will come down upon me, the gift of God's grace, which is not a spirit of timidity but a spirit of power and love and self-control (2 Tim 1:6, 7), the spirit that makes priests to offer sacrifice and witness to Your Word, the spirit that rescues us from ourselves and offers up our lives with Christ's sacrifice for the salvation of the world.

The bishop will lay his hands on me as in the Old Covenant hands were laid on a condemned man and on a sacrifice for expiating sin. For I am to follow Him whom You made sin for us, whereas He knew no sin (2 Cor 5:21), so that we might receive God's righteousness through Him; I am to follow the Lamb of God who took the world's sin upon Himself (John 1:29), upon whom You laid the guilt of us all (Isa 53:6). As Moses appointed Joshua leader of the people by laying hands on him, "and he was full of the spirit of wisdom, for Moses had laid hands on him" (Deut 34:9), as the Levites were appointed by the laying on of hands (Num 8:10), as Jesus laid his hands on children and the sick, as the Apostles laid hands on their disciples so that their Spirit passed to them when they set them apart for the work to which Your Spirit had called them and sent them forth (Acts 13:2, 3).

The bishop will lay hands on me and I shall be taken into the ranks of Your servants, who for two thousand years made their way through all ages and all lands to declare Your name before kings and nations. Into the unbroken chain that You began when Your Son our Lord said "Go into all the world . . . lo, I am with you"; into the unbroken chain of mission, of labor in a common destiny, of a new strength and power; into the one sacred race of Your priests that is renewed eternally not by blood and the will of the flesh but by birth of the Spirit and by the power of Your command; into the unbroken chain of Your priestly race which will never die out until You come to judge the living and the dead. The bishop will lay his hands on me. And then, still silent, he will take them from my head. But Your hand, O my God, will still remain upon me.

Your hands will remain upon me.

The hands of the Omnipotent, gentler than a mother's hands.

The hands that created and sustain all things.

The hands that can weigh heavy on a man and will often bear me down during my priestly life.

The hand that smites and heals.

The hands of the living God into which it is a dreadful thing to fall.

The hands into which at death I shall commend my spirit.

When Your hand, and so Your Spirit, rests upon me through the bishop's hand, then the prophecy of Isaiah will apply to me:

"The Spirit of the Lord God is upon me, because the Lord has anointed me to bring good tidings to the afflicted; he has sent me to bind up the broken-hearted, to proclaim liberty to the captives, and the opening of the prison to those who are bound, to proclaim the year of the Lord's favor" (Isa 91:1ff.).

Then I shall be able to say with Jesus, "Today this Scripture has been fulfilled in Your hearing" (Luke 4:21). Tomorrow, as with Timothy, my comrades in the army of the Lord will fraternally lay hands on me so that one Spirit and one power and one mission may live and work in all of us, so that the priestly spirit of Jesus' Church may be brought forth again. Then we shall belong to the presbyterate, be grown up, be among the elders. Then it will be our responsibility to see that the spirit of the Apostles and martyrs, the faithful, strong, selfless, believing, self-sacrificing spirit, the valiant, fighting, daring spirit that we receive, shall not die out.

Then the bishop will cross the stole over my breast, over my heart and clothe me with the vestment of a priest, the chasuble. Besides my baptismal robe, my God, You also give me the priestly robe. Let me bring both spotless to Your judgment seat. Of myself I am stark naked before You, for who is anything but nothingness and sin before Your incorruptible justice. But clothe me with the garment of justice and holy discipline. Prodigal son that I am, wrap me in the garments of Your grace, of everlasting light. And give me as well the armor of light (Rom 13:12) so that I shall be girt with truth, having on the breastplate of righteousness, shod with readiness to proclaim the gospel of peace, armed with the shield of faith, the helmet of salvation, and the sword of the word of God (see Eph 6).

Then the bishop will anoint my hands in the sign of the cross and bind them.

The hands that are to bless.

The hands that are to bestow God's peace on sinners.

The hands that will be extended in prayer for God's holy people.

The hands that are to hold the Lord's body and blood.

"Filling a man's hand," in the Old Covenant, meant ordaining him a priest. Fill my hands with Your blessing. Let them never be empty. Let them always be sanctified. Let them always be nimble in Your service and bound to Your command. Let them never reach out to evil. Let Your cross, the emblem of Your love, always burn on my hands like stigmata, so that I may always bear on my body the marks of Christ. As You anointed Aaron and his priests, kings and prophets, let me be anointed Your royal priest and prophet. Let me be anointed like Your Anointed, the Messiah, our Lord, "with the oil of gladness above my fellows," with the oil of strength and holiness, with the oil of the Holy Spirit, the oil of the godhead. With the anointing that abides in us, that teaches us about everything (1 John 2:27).

Then for the first time the bishop will entrust the paten and the chalice with the elements to my anointed hands. *Calicem salutaris accipiam et nomen Domini invocabo.* I shall hold the paten which is to bear the Lord's body. I shall grasp the chalice which contains the ransom for the sins of the world. I shall be Your priest. Tomorrow and every day of my life I shall celebrate the sacrifice of Christ. I shall be master of the word which turns the world into God. I shall offer the never-ending sacrifice of the new and eternal covenant. I shall hold in my hands the body that was delivered up for us. I shall lift the chalice with the blood that was redeemed and sanctified in the truth. I shall give my brethren Your body, the sacrament of grace, of the Lord's death, the sacrament of unity and love, the sacrament of the new body and of the resurrection. I shall be drawn, with my life, into Your death. I shall be Your priest.

Then, Lord Jesus Christ, You, a priest forever, will stand before me and look at me as You looked at Your Apostles, with a look of omniscience and unfathomable love, and say to me too: *Iam non dicam vos servos, sed amicos meos.* I have called you friends, for all that I have heard from my Father I have made known to you (John 15:15). Lord, I am Your servant and the son of Your handmaid, I am Your friend because You have said that I am and Your word is efficacious and almighty. I am Your friend because You have given me all You have—Your

Father, Your life, Your grace, Your command, Your authority, Your lot, Your cross, Your death, and Your eternal victory. And once more my holy exuberance is checked by Your sobering voice: *Vos amici estis, si feceritis quae ego praecipio vobis.* You are my friends if you do what I command you.

And then I shall say the creed once more, the "glorious confession before many witnesses" that Timothy made (1 Tim 6:13). The creed of the Apostles and of my ancestors and of my parents. The creed of my old dear childhood faith. The creed that gave joy to my youth. That I stood by as a man, that is better than all the wisdom of the world, that is God's word, that endures forever. The creed that my word, my labor, and my blood now belong to, that I am to speak and to live.

And once more the bishop will lay hands on me and tell me that I am sent to bind and to loose, to judge and to forgive in Your name. Let me always love this quiet, grave, humble office of forgiving sins. This office of the final deadly earnest of human life, sin. This office of Your inexhaustible pity and forbearance. This office in which Your justice and Your mercy, Your most human humanity and godliest godliness, become one. This office of keeping silence and being patient. This office of eternal life.

And finally the bishop will take my hands in his hands, and I shall promise the Church obedience and loyalty: exacting and unwavering obedience, selfless obedience, obedience whereby a man forgets his life in work that matters more than he does, obedience whereby a man loses himself only to find himself again in this steadfastness and constant generosity. Behold, I lay my hands in Your hands, my God. So take my hands and lead me: through joy and grief, through honor and disgrace, in labor and anguish, in my ordinary life and at great moments, in the holy stillness of Your house but also on the long, dusty roads of the world. Lead me today and always, lead me into the kingdom of Your eternal life.

When You have called and elevated me in this way, anointed me with power and sent me forth, I shall arise and walk again as Your priest for all eternity. Ordination to the priesthood is really Your last great word spoken in my life, Your last, crucial, final, irrevocable call. That shapes my life now for always. Whatever happens in my life now can only be my answer to, my living of, this final call, only a carrying out of this one final command that will rule my life always. Grant, therefore, that I may be found faithful. You have called me and You will see to it (1 Thess 5:24). For You do not repent of Your gifts. On the day of my ordination let the morning prayer of my priestly life be these words from the spirit of Ignatius, the holy warrior:

Eternal Word, only begotten Son of God,
Teach me true generosity.
Teach me to serve You as You deserve.
To give without counting the cost,
To fight heedless of wounds,
To labor without seeking rest,
To sacrifice myself without thought of any reward
Save the knowledge that I have done Your will.
Amen.

# PRAYER FOR THE RIGHT SPIRIT
# OF CHRIST'S PRIESTHOOD

Lord Jesus Christ, Son of the Living God, Eternal Word of the Father, High Priest of all men.

We thank You for being pleased to prepare us for Your priesthood.

We confess that *You* have chosen us, not we You, that without Your grace we should be unworthy and feeble and unfit to follow such a vocation. But You have prepared us. We are to be Your witnesses. We thank You, Angel of Great Counsel. We are to proclaim Your truth. We praise You, O Word of Eternal Truth. We are to renew Your sacrifice. We praise You, Priest and Victim forever. We are to dispense Your grace. We bless You, Incarnate Clemency of the Father, and give You heartfelt thanks for calling us into Your sanctuary, to Your altar, and to Your own priestly mission. We give You thanks. You spoke for us too when You came into the world. I too have come to do Your will, a body You have prepared for me. You besought God for us too when You prayed all night long for Your Apostles before choosing them. With us too You were patient and clement when You bore with Your uncomprehending disciples. You rejoiced over our work too when You blessed the Father at the disciples' homecoming. For us too You anxiously prayed that our faith should not waver and we should be strengthened in Peter, when Satan lusts to sift us like the wheat. We too were in Your mind when You gave the Apostles the law of their life in the Sermon on the Mount and the epitome of their prayer in the Our Father.

You included us when You said to Your Apostles: Let not your hearts be troubled; why are you afraid, O men of little faith? I appointed you that you should go and bear fruit, a servant is not greater than his master, whoever does not renounce all that he has cannot be my disciple. In Your Apostles You have called us Your friends, Your little children, Your brothers, as dear to You as brother and sister and mother. Your word was meant to reach our hearts too when You spoke these words to Your Apostles and a thousand more, which Your Gospel hands on to us as Your bequest to Your priests and which we should read on our knees and in tears. You have us too in mind when You uttered words before which all the principalities and powers of history quake and fall prostrate: Go and make disciples of all nations, baptizing them: do this in remembrance of me; if you forgive the sins of any, they are forgiven; whatever you loose on earth shall be loosed in heaven. O Jesus, Priest and King forever, it is Your will that we be and remain Your priests. Be blessed forever.

Lo, Lord, we would always be beginning anew to become what You have already called us to be. We shall go back joyful and courageous to the daily life where we are to mature still more into apostles and priests of Your holy Church. Give us Your Holy Spirit, therefore, and the spirit of Your priesthood for this new pilgrimage of ours, the spirit of reverence towards God, the spirit of contrition, the spirit of holiness and chaste fear of dishonoring the holy God by sin, the spirit of faith and love of prayer, the spirit of purity and manly discipline, the spirit of knowledge and wisdom, the spirit of brotherly love and concord beyond all envy and strife, the spirit of joy and confidence, the spirit of magnanimity and generosity, the spirit of obedience, patience, and love of Your holy cross. On this road let us have God Your Father before our eyes, let us walk in his holy presence, work honestly to teach our hearts, stick together among ourselves fraternally, share one another's burden and thus fulfill Your law.

Let us grow daily more and more like You through true, constant, selfless spiritual effort and struggle, O You the eternal wisdom of God!

Grant us, above all, the grace of prayer and make us love You, O Jesus. What are we without You? Lost. We can only have You if we make You, by love and prayer, again and again and more and more the focus of our heart. If You want us to be Your priests, then grant us, O Lord, that gift without which we cannot truly be Your priests. Grant us the grace of prayer, of collection, of inwardness, stop us when we want to run away from You in our distraction and absent-mindedness; bring us crazy people back to You, if need be by the prick of pain, the bitterness of heart and of distress. Give us just one gift: the grace to pray truly and to become daily more. When we pray, we are and remain in fellowship with You, then we shall increasingly become what we are and ought to be according to Your will: Your disciples, Your apostles, Your priests, the witnesses of Your truth and the dispensers of Your mysteries.

We have given ourselves and You the pledge to become Your priests: just priests and nothing besides, priests in undivided service. You look at us, Your eyes pierce through our conscience, Your love touches our heart. And You say: You are my friends if you do what I command you (John 15:14). But we dare to look up to You humbly and trustingly and to say: by Your grace we will be what You have commanded us to be.

Amen.

# THE SACRAMENT OF THE ALTAR

We kneel, Lord, before the Sacrament on the altars of Your holy Church, before the Sacrament of God's new and eternal covenant with the race of all the redeemed. We lift up our eyes to You, Lord, who are present among us in flesh and blood, body and soul, in divinity and humanity. We worship You, we bless You, we give You thanks. Present among us, You proclaim to us Your death: the night of the world, in which You were betrayed by us and by our sins; the transition of the world through death into the silent mystery of God. Your death is the sacrifice which reconciles heaven and earth, the sacrifice in which we are all sacrificed, given up to God, torn from ourselves, made a part of the transition and taken up also into the invisible burning flame of the spirit, which protects and sanctifies the world and brings it in salvation to God, even while it burns. We kneel Lord, before Your Sacrament, which unites us to You, to You the Son and the Eternal Word of the Father, to You, the Son of Man. When we eat this bread, we remain in You and You in us. When we receive You, You transform us into a part of Yourself, and faith, hope, and charity grow. When we have part in You, the Bread of Life and pledge of glory to come, we the many are one body; then either we eat judgment on our own selfishness or we receive the power of love, which frees, unites and includes everything. When we, as one holy community, raise You up as the sacrifice of the new covenant, when we receive You, then we show Your death until You come again, and You renew with us and in us the mystery of Your death. We are baptized into Your death. As often as we receive this Sacrament we acknowledge the mystery of Your death, which is life. You are in truth our bread, You who came among us in Your own Word, and You are in truth the Word in which the Father speaks to himself all truth for ever and ever. Live in us, who receive You, be to us the restless search for truth, the relentlessness of the highest truth in all human truth. Just as this bread is both the fulfillment of a sign and the veil of the eternal Word himself in this world of signs and images, so may human truth too, which we recognize and accept in our lives, be the sign and promise of eternal truth, which we hope one day to see face to face. When we receive You, come to us also as this truth of all truths. Come to us as the hope of eternal truth, which is eternal love. In the Sacrament of the Altar Your humanity is the pledge which unites us with Your divinity. Your humanity touches us and consecrates us. So may we, through this sacrament, become what we are: men, honest and true in body and soul, men in whom the presence of Your grace can find a symbol which will become effective for those whom we have to serve. Be for us who worship and receive You as the hidden, silent, sacrificed God of our life and death, a pledge of eternal life: the life of truth and of boundless freedom, the life of light and of undimmed brightness, the life in which we shall be blissfully consumed in adoration of the unsearchable God, the life in which all creatures will celebrate their blessed surrender to the Father, and God will become all in all. What we enact in the Church's sacrificial rite, in our adoration of this Sacrament, in the receiving of Your Body and Blood, will, by Your grace, always be enacted and celebrated in the sacred enactment of our own life, in its daily routines and in its climaxes, in life and in death. We ask the grace, that in this Sacrament You may be to us the food for our journey when we part from this world, when our death shall be taken up in Yours and the night will come when no one can be active any longer, when everything will sink into the nameless majesty of death. May we, who have celebrated Your redeeming death in the sacrament and the sacrifice of the Mass, proclaim it also through our own death. That Your death may become actual, as the power and constant meaning of our death, give us the grace to believe in Your Sacrament now, to celebrate it in hope and love, to set it up anew in the center of our lives on every Lord's Day and beyond. May Your Sacrament accompany us, Lord, on all this world's ways and lead us to the Kingdom of the Father, to Whom through You in the Holy Spirit be all honor and glory forever. Amen.

# THE EUCHARIST AND OUR DAILY LIVES

Come, Lord, enter my heart, You Who are crucified, Who have died, Who love, Who are faithful, truthful, patient, and humble, You Who have taken upon Yourself a slow and toilsome life in a single corner of the world, denied by those who are Your own, too little loved by Your friends, betrayed by them, subjected to the law, made the plaything of politics right from the very first, a refugee child, a carpenter's son, a creature who found only barrenness and futility as a result of his labors, a man who loved and who found no love in response, You Who were too exalted for those about You to understand, You Who were left desolate, Who were brought to the point of feeling Yourself forsaken by God, You Who sacrificed all, Who commend Yourself into the hands of Your Father, You Who cry: "My God, my Father, why have You forsaken Me?," I will receive You as You are, make You the innermost law of my life, take You as at once the burden and the strength of my life. When I receive You I accept my everyday just as it is. I do not need to have any lofty feelings in my heart to recount to You. I can lay my everyday before You just as it is, for I receive it from You Yourself, the everyday and its inward light, the everyday and its meaning, the everyday and the power to endure it, the sheer familiarity of it which becomes the hiddenness of Your eternal life.

# PRAYER OF A LAY PERSON

God, I always grow a bit uneasy whenever I hear the word "laity" in the Church. Ordinarily when one talks about "lay persons," one thinks of those who do not understand a certain matter or at least very little of it. But I have the right and obligation to understand as much as possible about the message of Jesus and His Kingdom, and it remains an unresolved question whether this should be any less than that possessed by those who enjoy full priestly authority in knowledge as well as in deed.

I definitely do not possess such authority, nor have I the slightest desire for it, because however much it is sought, it can only serve the same task which lies before me, namely, to be radically Christian, both as the Spirit of God moves me and as my life leads me closer to God in the discipleship of Jesus. In the final analysis, the clergy stand there too, not over me but next to me. God's grace not only comes to me through the sacramental signs which the clergy administer but remains above all else at the free disposal of God, who bestows it upon all who ask it of Him.

I know, Holy God, my responsibility as a Christian is a growing one. I must hold myself accountable for whether I allow the gifts and charisms by which I live to work sufficiently for others as well. I am not to preach in the pulpit but (a much more difficult thing) am to bear witness to the Gospel through my own example. In surroundings which neither outwardly reject nor truly desire Christianity, but which taboo the expression of anything religious, it becomes especially difficult to show who I am in the right place and at the right time and to take the position that a person has only truly made a commitment to his life when he decides to place himself in Your hands, O God, and dwell within Your grace.

More outspoken and less timid Christians testify to the fact that if one overcomes certain barriers, one's witness "opens doors" for others which heretofore appeared firmly closed. Why am I so fearful, so cowardly? And I must confess to being just that. Words such as "missionary," "apostolic," and so forth have to many people such a terribly old-fashioned ring. But what of the issue itself? And if it be absent, is that not an indication that the lay Christianity which I espouse is inherently wanting in strength?

O God, give me the courage and strength to be a lay person who is worthy of being called a Christian.

# PRAYER FOR
# JUSTICE AND BROTHERHOOD

I t is Your desire—it can be none other—that we ask of You
what our task is, what the plan for our own freedom is. For
it is we who have been Your partners throughout history, yet
only because You have ordained it so that our own work is
again Your grace and Your work. Hence we are as those who
execute what You have already done: God, may You be
thanked, for it would surely be an empty void, not to mention
an evil one, were we left alone to our own devices.

But, O Incomprehensible God, allow me to take up the cry
of pain and distress ringing on down through history: the
history of our deeds appears to us too blurred to be recognized
as part of *Your* inheritance. From the stone ax with which Abel
was slain up until the gas chambers in our own time—nothing
else but unmentionable cruelty, treachery, suffering, and death.

You will say, it is true, that all of this is the result of our
freedom, which I correctly admit, but reluctantly so. Yet, O
Incomprehensible God, it has been passed on to me from Saint
Paul by way of Saint Augustine and all of the great theologians
that even our freedom—harmful as it is, as far as I am concerned—is embraced by the power of Your unappealable will,
constrained by nothing, not even our freedom, and Your unfathomable predestination, which need not annul our freedom
in order to do in its freedom, also unconstrained by our freedom, that which pleases it to do.

I am telling this to myself (not to You!), not in order to sink
quickly before the incomprehensibility of Your will and Your
judgment, nor in order to defend Your absolute sovereignty

from the half-witted among us today who believe such a God cannot exist because He bursts all of our standards of measurement, so that once again Your unfathomableness falls, as I would see it, under the critique inaudible to us. I am only saying this in order to clarify for myself why I must call upon *You* for the justice and brotherhood which *we* must put into effect.

I know *we* must labor alone in the terrible struggle against our mostly hidden and legitimated egotism, in the vain hope of salvaging some trace of justice and brotherhood from our paltry hearts. I know too that I must cite myself and not others before Your judgment, when those virtues shall lead either to eternal salvation or to eternal ruin. And I also know that today a task of this sort can never simply be a private matter, a question of inward piety, but instead something born from the conditions of revolution, even as we must allow ourselves to be swayed by Jesus' command of nonviolence in His Sermon on the Mount. Yet it is true that we ought never shift the focus of our cause onto You, even in the midst of these troubled times in our history. In much the same way, I know that there can be no task of justice and brotherhood for us all which would not be the singular task of Your divine justice and brotherhood, that which You have endowed through Jesus Christ, Your Son and our brother.

For this reason, dare I utter the words: Give us what You hold before us, universal justice and brotherhood? I know that I must wait until the very end of human history before it will ever become clear to me that You hear and have heard my plea. But, pray forgive me, allow me even now to experience a little, a little more justice (or perhaps impartiality) and brotherhood. Go, You say, go and do that which You ask of me. It is then that I shall have done Your Will.

# PRAYER FOR PEACE

Holy Creator of the universe, of the earth and its people, it is Your will that humanity develop to the point where it is not only capable of committing, and continuing to commit, various and sundry evils but has the capacity to annihilate itself in an act of global suicide. Were You unable to prevent this possibility in the course of evolution, even if the history of humanity (we must ever be hopeful) shall still find its end in Your holy light and in Your peace in something greater than in all former stages of its development? Or is precisely this possibility alone a true confession of Who You are and who we are, as the culmination of God's creation moves inexorably toward that supreme descent into complete, even foreseeable, abomination.

Perhaps the very thought of global suicide does not make You shudder because You (one hopes, in Your merciful judgment) have looked upon the deed of Cain at the beginning and each and every suicide since throughout all the ages. But we, Your creatures, are not justified in willing this universal fratricide, this global suicide, or in tolerating it through our indolence. The possibility, not only the reality, exists which is so horrible, that even so much as a sluggish submission to it is deserving of punishment in Hell. You have allowed humanity to run astray in wholesale madness throughout history, wherefore nothing remains for us but to sink to our knees in tears before our God who created us.

And no one truly knows whether or not that which is most dreadful, that upon which Your searing judgment falls, occurs in the most dreadful human deeds or within the seemingly innocuous.

To that end, You have proclaimed (in such a way that we would have to take notice) that an end to human history is both Your will as well as Your plan of action. Yet, God, All-merciful One, am I actually to accept the fact that the end of humanity is to be brought about by an act of suicide? Even were we forced to submit such an act of lunacy to Your throne of judgment, this global suicide—an act perpetrated by so few but for which all are responsible—would be, objectively speaking, the gravest sin, the universal contradiction of Your will as Creator. This will desires that we exist and that we receive this very existence as the gift of Your boundless love.

God, such an act of suicide, surely, would be the one act of ours which would most repulse You. Our freedom, with all its shortsightedness and delusions, its insanities and hubris (allowing for the most extreme eventualities), nevertheless remains anchored in the sovereign power of Your freedom and of Your fathomless decree. God of Mercy, allow this small, pitiable creature to appeal to Your own sense of responsibility. It is indeed true that we ourselves must do everything possible to prevent the nuclear annihilation of all humankind from becoming not only a reality but (even more important!) a possibility, without resorting to the deadly hair-splitting on behalf of peace through nuclear balance of terror, without imagining that one might escape this ultimate horror by means of cooly reasoned discussion between the equally strong egos of the two superpowers, and, finally, without the audacious folly to be found in the Sermon on the Mount and in the love of Your only Son on the cross.

And yet, God of Mercy, I call upon You and Your mercy. If it be Your will, annihilate us and be rid of the sordid and sinful history of humanity once and for all. But did You allow the course of history to continue flowing through all these millennia merely to end it all, two thousand years after Your only Son achieved the reconciliation of the world on the cross, when, we may think, it is just now beginning to see the light of Your Gospel? Let humanity live so that it may in entirely new ways give You thanks for Your great glory.

Give all men the courage and valor to achieve peace and real disarmament. Give the Church the courage to teach not how one can cleverly reconcile the egotism among men, but rather how in light of the folly of the cross one can and indeed must assume direct responsibility for unconditional justice and peace. Convert the hearts of the mighty so that they may not yield to the deceitful pursuit of power in order to justify their own actions, nor deceive themselves and others while claiming to serve the ends of peace by proliferating arms. And ultimately: teach us within our own lives to further the cause of peace unselfishly.

# PRAYER FOR CREATIVE THINKERS

Eternal God, Creator of all men and of all things, invisible and visible alike, God of all history, You who are the Lord and the goal, the power and the light of all the activities of the human spirit, today we bring before You our prayer of intercession for all those who have a creative contribution to make in this field.

Lord, who else offers prayers on their behalf? And yet we know that the goal they set themselves, their creative power, their work and their achievements are willed by You. For Your will is extended unreservedly to those men who are engaged in constantly producing new expressions of their own nature and spirit, men who are the architects of themselves. You love the sort of man who realizes his own being in what he achieves and produces, who discovers and expresses that nature which is an image and likeness of Your own glory. That which Your will intends them to be, that they can only become with the help of Your grace, O Father of Poets, Eternal Source of all Light, Spirit of all True Inspiration!

It is for this, then, that we entreat You and invoke Your Holy Spirit upon them. Raise up among us men endowed with creative powers, thinkers, poets, artists. We have need of them! Remember that saying that man cannot live by bread of the body alone, that unless the word that proceeds from Your mouth becomes his nourishment he will go hungry. That saying applies to them too. Give to these young men the courage to respond to their inner call, to bear the burden and the pain which such a call involves, not to be led into betraying their task in the quest for money and the cheap applause of the superficial, who wish merely to be diverted. In words and in images, in their whole attitude and presentation they express what is in man because they proclaim what they themselves experience. And in expressing this let them express *everything*! Grant them the experience that man is not merely the frustrated hell of his own nothingness, but also the fair and blessed land over which stretches the heaven of Your own infinitude and freedom. They do not need to be constantly bringing You into everything they say. They must make mention of You by name only when they are filled with the spirit of the purest happiness or the deepest pain. For the rest let them honor You with their silence. For the rest let them praise the earth and humanity. But in doing this they must always bear You silently in their hearts, for it is here that their creative work has its source. Then even the slightest song becomes an echo of the rejoicing that takes place in Your heaven, and even when they have to tell of the most sombre depths to which man can sink, still their record of this is encompassed by Your compassion and permeated by a longing for light, virtue, and the eternal love. Then even an attempt to entertain is still a reflection of the gentleness and patience with which You love us in our daily lives. Give them the courage to attain to the light and to the joy in the darkness of this age and in all the hunger and poverty of our hearts. Such courage is a grace that comes from You. But give it to them, for we have need of such high courage. Give them the courage to distinguish and to decide. They do not need to be so very subtle, but their work must manifest the fact that an undivided heart has wrought them, one which, while it is open to everything, still in everything seeks You and seeks everything in You, recognizing no craven compromise of peace between the good and the evil, the light and the darkness. Give them the courage constantly to begin anew, because only so do they find their source in that which is true from all eternity. Let them say what *Your* Spirit has given into their hearts, rather than that which would make pleasant hearing to those who represent the forces of all that is average. When they make experience of the fact that all their work is in vain, of the frustration of their creativity and the insensitivity of their age, let them believe even then that in Your sight what seems to be so futile is not futile, that *You* have regarded their work with delight, and have gently taken their heart when it was breaking into Your own.

Your eternal Word, the effulgence of Your nature and the image of Your glory has Himself come in our flesh. He has taken upon Himself all that is human as *His own* reality. With a power that is greater and more ultimate, and a love that is deeper than that of any other creative worker for the work of his own hands He has set His own heart in the very center of the image His hands have wrought. He has done this in order that man himself may be the expression and the image of Your glory. And therefore, whether we realize it or not, every creative activity of the human spirit has become an element in the personal history of Your Word, because everything has come to belong to His own world, the world into which He came in order to share with it in its living experiences, to suffer with it and to glorify it with Himself. It is the world from which this Word of Yours will never more be separated for all eternity. Let those for whom we pray understand this truth. What they create is inevitably either a part of the Cross to which they nail Your Son in guilt, and therefore a condemnation of themselves, or else a factor contributing to the coming of the eternal Kingdom of this same Son, and therefore a grace for them. For this Kingdom does not only come from without as the end and the final judgment of this present world. It emerges as the hidden grace which has been present in the midst of this earthly reality ever since Your own Word descended into His own creation and became the heart of all things. Therefore everything which they create can and must be a promise that Your eternal Kingdom is already on the way, the Kingdom of truth and of love, the Kingdom of the glorification of man in his undivided nature, in body and soul, earth and heaven. Therefore grant to them too, that they may be proclaimers and promoters of this Kingdom. For everything which man himself has fashioned as sharer in Your creative power will be redeemed and taken into this Kingdom for all eternity, transferred and glorified. May the Spirit of Your Son come upon them in order that Your name may be praised now in this time and throughout all eternity.

Amen.

# MARY

Holy Virgin, truly mother of the eternal Word who has come into our flesh and our life, Lady who conceived in faith and in your blessed womb the salvation of us all, and so are the mother of all the redeemed, you who live ever in God's life, near to us still, because those united to God are nearest to us.

With the thankfulness of the redeemed, we praise the eternal mercy of God that redeemed you. When your existence began, sanctifying grace already was yours, and that irrevocable grace was with you always. You walked the way of all the children of this earth, the narrow paths which seem to wander so aimlessly through this life of time, commonplace, sorrowful roads, until death. But they were God's ways, the path of faith and unconditional consent: "Be it done unto me according to thy word." And in a moment that never passes, but remains valid for all eternity, your voice became the voice of all mankind, and your Yes was the Amen of all creation to God's irrevocable decree. You conceived in faith and in your womb Him who is at once God and man, creator and creature, changeless unalterable blessedness, and an earthly life marked out for bitter death, Jesus Christ our Lord. For our salvation you said Yes, for us you spoke your *Fiat*; as a woman of our race you accepted and bore in your womb and in your love him in whose Name alone there is salvation in heaven or on earth. Your Yes of consent ever remaincd, was never revoked, even when the course of the life and death of your Son fully revealed who it was that you had conceived: the Lamb of God, taking on himself the sins of the world; the Son of Man, nailed to the Cross by our sinful race's hatred of God, and thrown, Him the Light of the world, into the darkness of death, the lot that was ours. In you, holy Virgin, who stood under the Cross of the Redeemer (the real tree of the knowledge of good and evil, the real tree of life), as the second Eve and mother of all the living, it was redeemed humanity, the Church, that stood under the Cross and received the fruit of redemption and eternal salvation.

Here, virgin and mother, a congregation of the redeemed and the baptized has now gathered together. Here, then, where the communion of all the saints is visible and tangible, in this community, we ask you for your intercession. For the communion of saints includes those on earth and those who have attained their end and perfection, and in it none lives to himself alone. You do not do so either, then. You pray for all who are linked with you in this community as redeemed brothers and sisters. So we trustfully request your powerful intercession, which you do not refuse even to those who do not know you. You ask for grace for us to be true Christians: redeemed and baptized, more and more conformed to the life and death of our Lord, living in the Church in its Spirit, worshiping God in spirit and in truth, bearing witness to sanctifying grace through our life in all its branches, as human beings who are pure and chaste, truthful and seeking truth in everything, bravely and humbly giving shape and form to their life as a holy vocation from God, as children of God who, in the words of the apostle, are to "shine as lights in the midst of a crooked and perverse generation" (Phil 2:15), joyful and confident, their foundation the Lord of all the ages, today and for ever.

We consecrate ourselves to you, holy virgin and mother, because we are consecrated to you. Just as we are not only built up on the cornerstone Jesus Christ but also on the foundation of the apostles and prophets, so too our life and salvation is ever dependent on your consent, on your faith and the fruit of your womb. So when we say that we wish to be consecrated to you, we are only proclaiming our willingness to be, and to accept in mind and heart and action both interior and external, what we really are. By such a consecration we are only making the attempt to carry out in our own life-history the plan of redemption God laid down and in which he has already made his dispositions for us.

We come to you, then, because in you our salvation came to be, was conceived by you. Since we are consecrated to you thereby, and are consecrating ourselves to you, show to us who have been made sharers in your grace, Jesus the blessed fruit of thy womb. Show to us Jesus our Lord and Savior, the light of truth and the advent of God into this world of time. Show to us Jesus Who has truly suffered and truly risen, Who is the Son of the Father and the son of earth, because your Son. Show to us Him in Whom we are truly set free from all principalities and powers that are still under heaven, even though the man of earth is still subject to them. Show us Jesus Christ, yesterday, today, and for ever. Hail Mary, full of grace. . . .

Amen.

# PRAYER TO SAINT THOMAS AQUINAS

Saint Thomas, I must confess to you that at first it was somewhat difficult to hunt for and then to address one particular saint in the silent immeasurability of God (I could do it in relation to all the saints). But perhaps it is precisely that single correct choice that comes to one after much difficulty!

So I ask of you (using the traditional formula, the precise meaning of which I shall not ponder right at the moment): Grant that you will intercede for me with God, insofar as all saints stand for all other saints, among whom even poor sinners like myself belong—grant me your intercession so that even if only from afar I may become a little like you: impartial and sober, with the courage to consider well before delivering a fiery speech, a man of the Church but not clerical (my meaning here is doubtless clear to you).

And intercede also on behalf of two other matters: now you do virtually nothing but pray your *Adoro Te devote, latens Deitas* (I adore Thee, hidden Deity), for it is at this very moment that you behold the incomprehensibility of God, and it is no longer merely some abstract concept of your superior intellect, and you experience the act of silent worship in its pure origins in the power of the divine creativity, so that you forget yourself in the process of being intertwined with God and exactly so are yourself. Grant that whenever I am preaching, engaged in theology or in talking with people about God (Oh, such sublime torture), everything may be suffused (at the very least a little) with the awareness of that holy mystery which we call God, and of which you always said that it unfolds throughout all eternity ever more blissful as the adored and cherished mystery that saves us from our own narrow little corner.

And next: you remarked to your friend Reginald, What I have written is straw. You were modest and only spoke of what you had written yourself. And yet you cannot deny that such a statement holds true for everything that human beings can say about God, and that, provided one sees it, it is both the beginning and the promise of eternal life, wherein God satisfies without human words the insatiable longings of the spirit which derive from the grace of God.

# GOD OF THE LIVING

I should like to remember my dead to You, O Lord, all those who once belonged to me and have now left me. There are many of them, far too many to be taken in with one glance. If I am to pay my sad greeting to them all, I must rather travel back in memory over the entire route of my life's long journey.

When I look back in this way, I see my life as a long highway filled by a column of marching men. Every moment someone breaks out of the line and goes off silently, without a word or wave of farewell, to be swiftly enwrapped in the darkness of the night stretching out on both sides of the road. The number of marchers gets steadily smaller, for the new men coming up to fill the ranks are really not marching in my column at all.

True there are many others who travel the same road, but only a few are traveling with me. For the only ones making this pilgrimage with me are those with whom I set out together, the ones who were with me at the very start of my journey to You, my God, the dear ones who were, and still are, close to my heart.

The others are mere companions of the road, who happen to be going the same way as I. Indeed there are many of them, and we all exchange greetings and help each other along, But the true procession of my life consists only of those bound together by real love, and this column grows ever shorter and more quiet, until one day I myself will have to break off from the line of march and leave without a word or wave of farewell, never more to return.

That's why my heart is now with them, with my loved ones who have taken their leave of me. There is no substitute for them; there are no others who can fill the vacancy when one of those whom I have really loved suddenly and unexpectedly departs and is with me no more. In true love no one can replace another, for true love loves the other person in that depth where he is uniquely and irreplaceably himself. And thus, as death has trodden roughly through my life, every one of the departed has taken a piece of my heart with him, and often enough my whole heart.

A strange thing happens to the man who really loves, for even before his own death his life becomes a life with the dead. Could a true lover ever forget his dead? When one has really loved, his forgetting is only apparent; he only *seems* to get over his grief. The quiet and composure he gradually regains are not a sign that things are as they were before, but a proof that his grief is ultimate and definitive. It shows that a piece of his own heart has really died and is now with the living dead. This is the real reason he can weep no more.

Thus I am living now with the dead, with those who have gone before me into the dark night of death, where no man can work. But how can I really live with the dead? How can I continue to find life in the one bond left between us, the bond of our mutual love? Deign to answer me, O God, for You have called Yourself the God of the living and not of the dead. How can I live with them?

Of what use is it to say, as do the philosophers, that the dead still exist, that they live on? Are they with *me?* Since I loved them and still love them, I must be with them. But are they also with me?

They have gone away; they are silent. Not a word comes through from them; not a single sign of their gentle love and kindness comes to warm my heart. How awfully still the dead are, how *dead!* Do they want me to forget them, as one forgets a fleeting acquaintance he made on a train, a stranger with whom he once exchanged a few friendly but meaningless words?

If it's true that those who have departed in Your love have not really lost their life, but have had it transformed into eternal, limitless, superabundant life, why then do I perceive no sign? Why are they for me as if they were no more? Is the eternal light into which they have entered—which is Your light, my God—so feeble that its rays can't reach down to me? Must not only their bodies, but also their love depart from me, in order to be with You? My question thus turns away from them to You, my God, for You want Yourself to be called the God of the living and not of the dead.

But why am I asking this of You? You are as silent to me as my dead. I love You too, as I love my dead, the quiet and distant ones who have entered into night. And yet not even You give me answer, when my loving heart calls upon You for a sign that You and Your Love are present to me. So how can I complain about my dead, when their silence is only the echo of Yours? Or can it be that Your silence is Your answer to my complaint about theirs?

That must be the way it is, since You are the last answer, even though incomprehensible, to all the questions of my heart. I know why You are silent: Your silence is the framework of my faith, the boundless space where my love finds the strength to believe in Your Love.

If it were all perfectly evident to me here on earth, if Your Love of me were so manifest that I could ask no more anxious questions about it, if You had made absolutely crystal clear the most important thing about me, namely, that I am someone loved by You, how then could I prove the daring courage and fidelity of my love? How could I even have such love? How could I lift myself up in the ecstasy of faith and charity, and transport myself out of this world into Your world, into Your Heart?

Your Love has hidden itself in silence, so that my love can reveal itself in faith. You have left me, so that I can discover You. If You were with me, then in my search for You I should always discover only myself. But I must go out of myself, if I am to find You—and find You there, where You can be Yourself.

Since Your Love is infinite, it can abide only in Your Infinity; and since You will to manifest Your infinite Love to me, You have hidden it in my finiteness, where You issue Your call to me. My faith in You is nothing but the dark path in the night between the abandoned shack of my poor, dim earthly life and the brilliance of Your Eternity. And Your silence in this time of my pilgrimage is nothing but the earthly manifestation of the eternal word of Your Love.

That is how my dead imitate Your silence: they remain hidden from me because they have entered into Your life. The words of their love no longer reach my ears, because they are conjoined with the jubilant song of Your endless Love. My dead live the unhampered and limitless Life that You live; they love with Your Love; and thus their life and their love no longer fit into the frail and narrow frame of my present existence. I live a dying life—*prolixitas mortis* is the Church's name for this life—so how can I expect to experience their eternal life, which knows no death?

And that is also the way they live for me. Their silence is their loudest call to me, because it is the echo of Your silence. Their voice speaks in unison with Yours, trying to make itself heard above the noisy tumult of our incessant activity, competing with the anxious protestations of mutual love with which we poor humans try to reassure each other. Against all this, their voice and Yours strive to enwrap us and all our words in Your eternal silence.

Thus Your word summons us to enter into Your Life. Thus You command us to abandon ourselves by the daring act of love which is faith, so that we may find our eternal home in Your Life. And thus I am called and commanded by the silence of my dead, who live Your Life and therefore speak Your word to me, the word of the God of Life, so far removed from my dying. They are silent because they live, just as we chatter so loudly to try to make ourselves forget that we are dying. Their silence is really their call to me, the assurance of their immortal love for me.

O Silent God, God of the silent dead, Living God of the living, who call to me through silence, O God of those who are silently summoning me to enter into Your Life, never let me forget my dead, my living. May my love and faithfulness to them be a pledge of my belief in You, the God of eternal life.

Let me not be deaf to the call of their silence, which is the surest and sincerest word of their love. May this word of theirs continue to accompany me, even after they have taken leave of me to enter into You, for thus their love comes all the closer to me. O my soul, never forget Your dead, for they live. And the life they live, now unveiled in eternal light, is Your own life, which will one day be revealed also in You.

O God of the living, may Your living not forget me, as I still walk in the valley of death. You have granted them everything, even Yourself; grant them this too, that their silence may become the most eloquent word of their love for me. May it lead me home to the Kingdom they now possess, to the life and light they now enjoy.

My waning life is becoming more and more a life with the dead. I live more and more with those who have gone before me into the dark night where no man can work. By Your life-giving grace, O Lord, let it become ever more a life of faith in Your light, shining now dimly in this earthly night. Let me live with the living who have preceded me in the sign of faith, who have gone before me into the bright day of eternal life, when no man need work, because You Yourself are this day, the Fullness of all Reality, the God of the Living.

When I pray, "Grant them eternal rest, O Lord, and let Thy perpetual light shine upon them," let my words be only the echo of the prayer of love that they themselves are speaking for me in the silence of eternity: "O Lord, grant unto him, whom we love in Your Love now as never before, grant unto him after his life's struggle Your eternal rest, and let Your perpetual light shine also upon him, as it does upon us."

O my soul, never forget the dead. O God of all the living, do not forget me, the dead one, but come one day to be my life, as You are theirs.

# GOD WHO IS TO COME

E very year Your Church celebrates the holy season of Advent, my God. Every year we pray those beautiful prayers of longing and waiting, and sing those lovely songs of hope and promise. Every year we roll up all our needs and yearnings and faithful expectation into one word: "Come!"

And yet, what a strange prayer this is! After all, You have already come and pitched Your tent among us. You have already shared our life with its little joys, its long days of tedious routine, its bitter end. Could we invite You to anything more than this with our "Come?" Could You approach any nearer to us than You did when You became the "Son of Man," when You adopted our ordinary little ways so thoroughly that it's almost hard for us to distinguish You from the rest of our fellow men?

In spite of all this we still pray: "Come." And this word issues as much from the depth of our hearts as it did long ago from the hearts of our forefathers, the kings and prophets who saw Your day still far off in the distance, and fervently blessed its coming. Is it true, then, that we only "celebrate" this season, or is it still really Advent?

Have You really already come? Was it really You, the God we were expecting when we poured forth our longing for "Him who was to come," for the Mighty God, Father of the Future, Prince of Peace, the God of Light and Truth and Eternal Happiness? Indeed, Your coming is promised in the very first pages of Holy Scripture, and yet on the last page, to which no more will ever be added, there still stands the prayer: "Come, Lord Jesus!"

Are You the eternal Advent? Are You He who is always still to come, but never arrives in such a way as to fulfill our expectations? Are You the infinitely distant One, who can never be reached? Are You the One toward whom all races and all ages, all the longings of all men's hearts must plod on eternally over never-ending highways?

Are You only the distant horizon surrounding the world of our deeds and sufferings, the horizon which, no matter where we roam, is always just as far away? Are You only the eternal Today, containing within itself all time and all change, equally near to everything, and thus also equally distant?

Is it that You don't want to come, because You still possess what we were yesterday and today are no more, and have already gone infinitely beyond what we shall be in the farthest future? When our bleeding feet have apparently covered a part of the distance to Your eternity, don't You always retreat twice as far away from us, into the immense reaches filled only by Your Infinite Being? Has humanity drawn the least bit closer to You in the thousands and thousands of years that have elapsed since it boldly began its most exciting and fearsome adventure, the search for You?

Have I come any nearer to You in the course of my life, or doesn't all the ground I have won only make my cup all the more bitter, because the distance to You is still infinite? Must we remain ever far from You, O God of Immensity, because You are ever near to us, and therefore have no need of "coming" to us? Is it because there is no place in Your world to which You must first "find Your way?"

You tell me that You have really already come, that Your name is Jesus, Son of Mary, and that I know in what place and at what time I can find You. That's all true, of course, Lord— but forgive me if I say that this coming of Yours seems to me more like a going, more like a departure than an arrival.

You have clothed Yourself in the form of a slave. You, the hidden God, have been found as one of us. You have quietly and inconspicuously taken Your place in our ranks and marched along with us. You have walked with us, even though we are beings who are never coming, but rather always going, since any goal we reach has only one purpose: to point beyond itself and lead us to the last goal, our end.

And thus we still cry: "Come! Come to us, You who never pass away, You whose day has no evening, whose reality knows no end! Come to us, because our march is only a procession to the grave." Despairing of ourselves, we call upon You— then most of all, when, in composure and quiet resignation, we bring ourselves to accept our finiteness.

We have called out to Your Infinity—Its coming is the sole

hope we have of attaining unending life. For we have learned—at least those of us to whom You have granted the gift of knowing the final meaning of this life—that our search was in vain, that we were seeking the impossible. We had thought to escape by our own power from the strangling anxiety of being frail and transitory. We had hoped by a thousand different methods of our own clever devising to run away from our own being, and thus become masters of an eternal existence.

But bitter experience has taught us that we cannot help ourselves, that we are powerless to redeem ourselves from ourselves. And so we have called upon Your Reality and Your Truth; we have called down upon ourselves the Plenitude of Your Life. We have made appeal to Your Wisdom and Your Justice, Your Goodness and Your Mercy. We have summoned You, so that You Yourself might come and tear down the barriers of our finiteness, and turn our poverty into riches, our temporality into eternity.

You promised that You would come, and actually made good Your promise. But how, O Lord, how did You come? You did it by taking a human life as Your own. You became like us in everything: born of a woman, You suffered under Pontius Pilate, were crucified, died, and were buried. And thus You took up again the very thing we wanted to discard. You began what we thought would end with Your coming: our poor human kind of life, which is sheer frailty, finiteness, and death.

Contrary to all our fond hopes, You seized upon precisely this kind of human life and made it Your own. And You did this not in order to change or abolish it, not so that You could visibly and tangibly transform it, not to divinize it. You didn't even fill it to overflowing with the kind of goods that men are able to wrest from the small rocky acre of their temporal life, and which they laboriously store away as their meager provision for eternity.

No, You took upon Yourself our kind of life, just as it is. You let it slip away from You, just as ours vanishes from us. You held on to it carefully, so that not a single drop of its torments would be spilled. You hoarded its every fleeting moment, so You could suffer through it all, right to the bitter end.

You too felt the inexorable wheel of blind, brute nature rolling over Your life, while the clear-seeing eye of human malice looked on in cruel satisfaction. And when Your humanity glanced upward to the One who, in purest truth and deepest love, it called "Father," it too caught sight of the God whose ways are unfathomable and whose judgments are incomprehensible, who hands us the chalice or lets it pass, all according to His own holy Will. You too learned in the hard school of suffering that no "why" will ever ferret out the secret of that Will, which could have done otherwise, and yet chose to do something we would never understand.

You were supposed to come to redeem us from ourselves, and yet You, who alone are absolutely free and unbounded, were "made," even as we are. Of course, I know that You remained what You always were, but still, didn't our mortality make You shudder, You the Immortal God? Didn't You, the Broad and Limitless Being, shrink back in horror from our narrowness? Weren't You, Absolute Truth, revolted at our pretense?

Didn't You nail Yourself to the cross of creation, when You took as Your own life something which You had drawn out of nothing, when You assumed as Your very own the darkness that You had previously spread out in eternal distance as the background to Your own inaccessible light? Isn't the Cross of Golgotha only the visible form of the cross You have prepared for Yourself, which towers throughout the spaces of eternity?

Is that Your real coming? Is that what humanity has been waiting for? Is that why men have made the whole of human

history a single great Advent-choir, in which even the blas-
phemers take part—a single chant crying out for You and Your
coming? Is Your humble human existence from Bethlehem to
Calvary really the coming which was to redeem wretched
humanity from its misery?

Is our grief taken from us, simply because You wept too? Is
our surrender to finiteness no longer a terrible act of despair,
simply because You also capitulated? Does our road, which
doesn't want to end, have a happy ending despite itself, just
because You are traveling it with us?

But how can this be? And why should it be? How can our life
be the redemption of itself, simply because it has also become
Your life? How can You buy us back from the Law, simply by
having fallen under the Law Yourself (Gal. 4:5)?

Or is it this way: is my surrender to the crushing narrowness
of earthly existence the beginning of my liberation from it,
precisely because this surrender is my "Amen" to Your human
life, my way of saying "Yes" to Your human coming, which
happens in a manner so contrary to my expectations?

But of what value is it to me that my destiny is now a participation in Yours, if You have merely made mine Your own?
Or have You made my life only the *beginning* of Your coming,
only the starting point of Your life?

Slowly a light is beginning to dawn. I'm beginning to understand something I have known for a long time: You are still in
the process of Your coming. Your appearance in the form of a
slave was only the beginning of Your coming, a beginning in
which You chose to redeem men by embracing the very slavery
from which You were freeing them. And *You* can really
achieve Your purpose in this paradoxical way, because the
paths that *You* tread have a real ending, the narrow passes
which *You* enter soon open out into broad liberty, the cross

that *You* carry inevitably becomes a brilliant banner of triumph.

Actually You haven't come—You're still coming. From Your Incarnation to the end of this era is only an instant, even though millennia may elapse and, being blessed by You, pass on to become a small part of this instant. It is all only the one, single moment of Your single act, which catches up our destiny into Your own human life, and sweeps us along to our eternal home in the broad expanses of Your divine Life.

Since You have already begun this definitive deed, Your final action in this creation, nothing new can really happen any more. Our present era is the last: in the deepest roots of all things, time is already standing still. "The final age of the world has come upon us" (1 Cor 10:11). There is only a single period left in this world: Your Advent. And when this last day comes to a close, then there will be no more time, but only You in Your Eternity.

If deeds measure time, and not time deeds—if one new event ushers in a new age, then a new age, and indeed the last, has dawned with Your Incarnation. For what could still happen, that this age does not already carry in its womb? That we should become partakers of Your Being? But that has already happened, the moment You deigned to become partaker of our humanity.

It is said that You will come again, and this is true. But the word *again* is misleading. It won't really be "another" coming because You have never really gone away. In the human existence which You made Your own for all eternity, You have never left us.

But still You will come again, because the fact that You have already come must continue to be revealed ever more clearly. It will become progressively more manifest to the world that the heart of all things is already transformed, because You have taken them all to Your Heart.

You must continue to come more and more. What has already taken place in the roots of all reality must be made more and more apparent. The false appearance of our world, the shabby pretense that it has not been liberated from finiteness through Your assuming finiteness into Your own life, must be more and more thoroughly rooted out and destroyed.

Behold, You come. And Your coming is neither past nor future, but the present, which has only to reach its fulfillment. Now it is still the one single hour of Your Advent, at the end of which we too shall have found out that You have really come.

O God who is to come, grant me the grace to live now, in the hour of Your Advent, in such a way that I may merit to live in You forever, in the blissful hour of Your Eternity.

# BETWEEN GRACE AND JUDGMENT

Lord Jesus Christ, I have heard Your word of forgiveness in the Sacrament. I have heard once again what we cannot hear too often: that You will be merciful and forgive me. Time and time again. With inexhaustible patience, forbearingly and faithfully. I thank You for Your goodness, for the magnanimity and patience which You have shown me all the days of my life. In this sacrament I experience Your grace again and again. I receive Your forgiveness, freely granted, to meet my daily need. I need Your grace and love again and again in the

confessional; grant that I may bring the message of that grace
and love to my neighbor in his need. Grant too that I may share
his burden by my prayers; that I may be patient and knowing,
humble and wise, an apostle, preaching Your word so that it
may penetrate and convert all hearts. Count me with those
who receive and hand on the peace of Your forgiveness. May
the merciful judgment of Your grace, which I receive in the
Sacrament of Penance, forever be a promise of that judgment
which I am to meet, of the Last Judgment, which will conclude
and fulfill all the judgments of this time, both in the sacrament
and in our lives. I am already approaching this judgment. "It is
appointed unto men once to die, and after this the judgment"
(Heb 9:27). How near, O Lord, am I already to that day; how
very near to the moment when I will be parted from all that
I do not wish to part from, the moment which comes but once
and which we must face alone. Only for three hours do I hang
beside You, as a poor thief, on the cross of this world and this
age: a short life. Shall I have used it to say to You: Lord,
remember me when You come into Your Kingdom? Shall I
have used it, this fleeting moment that I call my life, to put my
poor soul into Your Father's hand, freely, in faith and love?
Shall I have acted in such a way that the words: "It is a fearful
thing to fall into the hands of the living God" (Heb 10:31) will
not refer to me? Lord, when You come lika a thief in the night,
do not judge me. I do not know when You are coming, I only
know that You will come soon. When You come, come in the
gentle secrecy of Your grace before You come as judge. Kindle
and leave burning in my heart the light of faith and the fire of
Your love. Before You come as judge, prepare for me the house
of my eternity, in which You will live, and see that it is in
order and worthy to become my only heaven and Yours. Give
me the grace of perseverance. This is what You give, when You
give me the grace of unwavering trust in Your mercy, when

You give me the grace to believe that You are greater than our hearts, when You give me the grace of prayer and of love. You give me the grace of perseverance, in giving me the grace to forget my own willfulness in the holy mission which You have entrusted to me, in the holy destiny to which You have called me. You give it to me in the grace to love and honor Your Sacred Heart and your mother and mine.

I kneel, O Lord, before Your sacrament which proclaims Your death. If I remain united to You in faith, hope, and charity, it proclaims my death also. For then I shall live and die in You. In Baptism I was baptised into Your death sacramentally; when I come to die I shall be united with Your death in sober reality, for You have shared my death. Give me Your death, the most personal death that a man can die. If it is Your will, give me at the hour of death Your sacrament as food for the journey and as a final pledge of eternal life. But I implore You, be near me in that hour, in the sacrament or without that outward sign; if it is Your will, let me share Your mortal loneliness and desolation, the infinite weakness which You knew at the hour of death, but whatever happens, give me then Your grace and Your eternal life. Lord, You have died for us. You died for every human creature as though for him alone. Remember this always, and especially at the hour of our death. If You forget none of us, then every death will be a participation in Your death and every judgment the eternal victory of Your mercy.

Amen.

# THE RESURRECTION OF THE DEAD

My God, whenever I start to listen more carefully to that hope for eternity that lives within me, it is then that I become acutely aware of an odd difficulty: on the one hand, I do not enjoy talking about the "soul," which, initially at least, enters alone through the gates of death into Your life, nor about the immortality of the soul, for I experience myself too "bodily" for that (not to mention other theological problems). But on the other hand, I continue to imagine my own "afterlife" (which I do believe in) as something quite abstract and de-mythologized: what shall I do with heavenly clouds and the last trumpet, multitudes gathering in the valley of Jehoshapat, the opening of tombs, and so on? My conception of the here-after appears to have shrunk to the conviction that even in death I will remain sheltered in Your power and love and bliss without knowing how this is so. And even these words, which are an expression of my faith, I must again qualify with the label "analogy."

Is my belief in the herafter, my certainty of the "resurrection of the dead," actually real? Must I harbor the suspicion that I am a rationalist with an ever diminishing faith? You appear to remain silent and to abandon me to my own wavering notions. Now, I may perhaps think this way: if I "deny" this or that about You or about the hereafter and the resurrection (I don't separate these two things, entrusting that task to more astute theologians), then I may affirm this denial in a positive way—this denial which separates things and ideas from You and the resurrection because they don't seem to fit the preconceived meaning (if I do have a "body" in Heaven, on what kind of a chair shall I sit?)—because Your infinite reality and power has no need to deny these apparently denied realities, but rather raises them up and preserves them in a sublime way.

To my mind, it is far too easy a thing to willingly abandon the "material" because it simply cannot be affirmed of You and so to affirm the "spiritual"—of You and of our consummation—as if it had not to be conceived in a wholly different manner, should it be affirmed at all. "Spirit" and "matter" must certainly be taken up in a totally different, changed way in an affirmation about You and about our consummation. But "matter"(completely altered and changed) can also be really affirmed of You and of our consummation, since You are once again exalted above and beyond our distinctions and abstractions. You are unimaginably close to that which we (with some justification) perceive as infinitely far away, for You are not merely the "Superior Being" but the Author and Source of all things. Were not matter in some sense similar to You, You could scarcely create it and, as many ancient philosophers thought, it would hence be conceived of as the "Antidivine."

For this reason, I await with joy the resurrection and consider that doctrine not as an affirmation of some secondary particle of the world, but as the basic affirmation of the fact that You do not confront matter in a hostile and merely negative way, but instead have constituted it as the common source of all reality unfolding upward toward the Spirit (in Your power naturally), a reality in which even the angels are deeply rooted. And whenever in praise of the absoluteness of our existence we speak about our surroundings, about seeing, about dancing, about blissful rejoicing, about tasting or about touching, it is at that point that I am no longer sure how all this has its place next to and along with the direct vision of Your eternally incomprehensible reality and glory. But I really mustn't attenuate these hard sayings along esoteric lines, like all those statements of a spiritual-metaphysical sort which only seem easier to understand. When the consummation comes, we will be amazed at how totally different everything is from what we had ever imagined it to be (as well as how far from reality are the illusions of spiritualists). Yet it is just this total difference which shows itself so strikingly close to and congruent with our whole existence up till now. My spirit and my flesh will exult in God my Savior. Since in the eternity of God time no longer plays a role for us, the question of whether or not a disparity exists (inviting comparison with our own time) between that which we call our personal spiritual consummation and that which is known as the resurrection doesn't interest me in the slightest.

I wait, O God, with patience and in hope. I wait like a blind man who has been promised the dawning of light. I await the resurrection of the dead and of the flesh.

# A BLESSING ON OUR ENDING

Lord Jesus Christ, the ending of any task leads us to You just as much as its beginning, for You are beginning and end.

This ending of ours, Lord, is but a small beginning, our mission and not its achievement, our good resolutions and not their fulfillment. But You have given us the beginning. Of You it is written: "He is faithful who hath called you, who also will do it" (1 Thess 5:24). Therefore we ask You: grant us Your grace in full measure, as we now try again to carry out the life and the mission You have entrusted to us.

It is the same old world which lies in wait for us, O Lord, the same as ever: our own weakness and sinfulness, the old familiar surroundings, the same daily round, the darkness of the future today as yesterday, our same consciousness of the Old Adam in us. This is why we have no faith in ourselves or our good resolutions, in our enthusiasm or even in our strength of purpose. But we do have faith in Your grace, in Your forbearance and patience with us. Only stay with us, O Lord; stay with us through the day and when it is toward evening. We do not ask that Your continuing presence should be reflected for us in lofty emotions, for these only reflect ourselves, not You. We can believe without these that You are with us all days even unto the end, when the bitter cup of Your death must be drained. You are with us; that suffices. Stay with us: this is our plea. Stay with us, in Your Holy Spirit, in the Spirit of the fear of God, in the Spirit of contrition, humility and chaste fear lest we dishonor the holiness of God by sin, in the Spirit of faith and of the love of prayer, in the Holy Spirit of courage and of responsibility for Your gospel and for Your Kingdom in this world and in our time, in the Spirit of generosity and magnanimity, in the grace of the love of Your holy Cross. Time and again You become the holy Bread for us, pilgrims between time and eternity. Grant then that we may receive You with sincere faith and true love, You, the Lord of our lives and source of all grace, our strength in dying, our pledge of eternity, and the holy bond of love between us, Your brothers. Give us the grace to recognize all that crosses the plans and calculations of our life as Your Cross and as a sharing in Your death, which reveals true life. Fill our hearts with the power of Your eternal victory and with the blind trust that Your Kingdom will last forever and will rise victorious where we are only conscious of apparent defects.

Lord, You see that we ask but for one thing: that You will

stay with us and that we may always imitate You. We ask You to give us only what You have already given us, to complete what You Yourself have begun. We ask You for only one thing: for You Yourself. Since You are in truth the love of God incarnate, we know that You hear our prayer. You gave Yourself to us, You even fixed Your destiny and Your life in the history of the world and humanity, You became our friend and brother, the true companion of our existence and our destiny. You became like us in everything. So it does not offend You to be with us and to regard our cause as Your cause. You always hear our prayer; and our prayer for Your continuing presence in us is the first-fruit of Your presence in us now.

To You is entrusted all that we have and are: our salvation, our vocation, our daily work, our families, our life and our death. So at the end, O Lord, our prayer is the sum of all desire and of all prayer: Take and receive, O Lord, my whole freedom, my memory, my understanding and my whole will, all that I have and possess. From You it came, Lord, to You I offer it all again. All is Yours, dispose of it entirely according to Your will. Give me only Your love and Your grace, for that is enough.

Amen.

# PRAYER FOR THE REUNION OF ALL CHRISTIANS

God, cause and moving force of all unity, we cry out to You and ask You to grant the Christian churches which are separated from each other that unity which conforms to the will of our Lord, Jesus Christ. We know, of course, that we ourselves have to do all that is possible for us to make this unity a reality, for the split between the Christian churches came about through us, not through You. But precisely this task of ours is nevertheless the gift of Your grace which alone can grant the desire for and the achievement of that unity. And therefore all our efforts can begin again and again only with the prayer: grant what You ask of us.

When all Christian churches profess a triune God, one Lord and Redeemer Jesus Christ, when we are all baptized into You, the triune God, and are born again to eternal life in the power of Your divine Spirit, Who (so we hope) has already taken possession of us in the depth of our being, then there already does exist among us Christians that divine unity which You Yourself are; and when we pray for the unity which is yet to come, then we mean a unity of churches as an embodied historical fact, which has its source in that ultimate unity which is already given as testimony to the world and in history that the One Church can truly and clearly be the sacrament of redemption of the world.

The unity of the churches is our task. And therefore we ask: may Your Spirit fill all the churches with a healing fear concerning that which all churches (different but without exception) have inflicted on the Body of Your Son, Who is the Church; inflicted through lust of power, arrogance, infatuation with one's own opinion, lack of loving tolerance, narrowness of mind which will not allow Your One Truth to be proclaimed with many tongues, and through all other ways in which we human beings are sinners and put ourselves in place of Your Truth.

Grant us the foresight and wisdom in our powerless activity so that we do not cause yet more division within the churches through our arrogant zeal for unity. Make the leaders of the churches clearsighted and courageous so that they feel more of a responsibility to the unity of the churches in the future than to the independence of their churches in the past. Make them daring because in the history of the Church something that is really new and great arises only when it is not completely legitimized by the past alone. Give them the joyous conviction that much more from the past can be gathered into the One Church by all the churches than is thought possible by a vision made shortsighted and fearful by the fact that what is to be gathered in was once the cause of division. Grant those in positions of responsibility in the Church the conviction that unity does not mean uniformity, by which one Church alone becomes the complete law for all the others, but rather reconciled diversity of the churches.

Everyone in the separated churches must grant his Christian brothers in the other churches good intentions to fulfill Jesus' demand for unity among his disciples, and yet we sinners in all churches must confess that these intentions are obviously not yet as glowing, courageous, and creative among us as they should be. For otherwise that unity which is our task should have come true already. Holy and Merciful God, grant us the full intention for unity which You demand of us. And, if our heart accuses us of possessing too little of the powerful Spirit of Unity, then we may nevertheless hope that this sinful weakness of ours remains enveloped by Your mercy and in that unity of Christians which You already bestowed on us.

Amen.

# CLOSING

My brothers and sisters, let us close on a quiet note, so that God's gentle yet powerful word of grace within us is not drowned by our loud and weak human words. Let us pray: "Lord, help my unbelief," give me the grace of faith in Jesus Christ our Lord, in his gospel and his saving power.

# EDITOR'S AFTERWORD

Prayers may be found among Karl Rahner's earliest publications. The collection *Worte ins Schweigen* (*Encounters with Silence*), which appeared in book form in 1938 and shortly afterward in several editions and later in a number of translations, belongs to the period of the author's involvement with philosophy.[1] In 1936, work was completed on *Geist in Welt* (*Spirit in the World*), which deals with the Thomistic metaphysics of knowledge, and the first edition appeared in 1939. The second, larger collection of reflective prayers appeared in 1949 under the title *Heilige Stunde und Passionsandacht* (*Watch and Pray with Me*). In 1958, together with his brother Hugo, Karl Rahner published the slim volume *Gebete der Einkehr* (*Prayers for Meditation*). It contains texts that were first delivered at a student mission held in the Freiburg cathedral in 1951 and which were subsequently incorporated into several prayers "which sought to express in words the dialogue between the soul and God according to the Spiritual Exercises of St. Ignatius Loyola."[2] In this manner they were often recited during the various retreats that Rahner gave based

[1]For a biography of Karl Rahner, see Karl Lehmann, "Karl Rahner, Ein Porträt," in *Rechenschaft des Glaubens: Karl Rahner-Lesebuch,* ed. Karl Lehmann and Albert Raffelt (Zurich/Freiburg, 1979) 13-46.
[2]Karl Rahner, in the preface to Karl Rahner and Hugo Rahner, *Worte ins Schweigen, Gebete der Einkehr* (Freiburg, 1973) 7.

on the Exercises (see, for example, his *Betrachtungen zum ignatianischen Exerzitienbuch*, 1965[3]). Although Rahner produced no other collection of prayers since that time, individual prayers again and again constitute part of his spiritual writings and are closely linked to his academic theological work. An especially fitting example would be the three short "Prayers of Recollection"[4] that originally had been the closing words for three Advent sermons which Rahner delivered in the Münster cathedral in 1967 at the invitation of the Catholic Students' Association. They were published the following year in the book *Ich glaube an Jesus Christus*, which may be considered one of Rahner's most significant and impressive publications on christology. The list of Sources which follows indicates in detail from which publications these and the remaining prayers were taken. Additional, hitherto unpublished writings from the more recent period have also been included.

This brief survey shows plainly that the individual prayers came about over a period of many years and arose in a variety of contexts. That Rahner's religious vocabulary changed considerably within the course of almost a half century needs little further explanation. No attempt has been made to conceal this aspect of these writings by revising the text.

For the reader who is interested in theology, it might prove stimulating to examine the relationship of these prayers to Rahner's theological writings. What is most apparent is that the earliest texts offer parallels to Rahner's philosophical inquiries into the transcendental approach to knowledge. Moreover, from their side they may help to clarify the "spiritual locus" of corresponding reflections on the problem of the knowledge of God. A comparison of the previously mentioned "Prayers of Recollection" might well prove decisive in understanding the development of Rahner's work in christology.[5]

---

[3]The English edition, *Spiritual Exercises*, translated by Kenneth Baker (New York: Herder and Herder, 1965) does not include these prayers.— Translator.

[4]Here under the titles: "Following Christ Through Love of Neighbor," "God's Word as Personal Promise," and "Meeting Jesus."

[5]See also Rahner's brief comments in *Karl Rahner: Im Gespräch*, vol. 1 (Munich: 1982) 240-242.

Nevertheless, the aim of this collection is not to provide a manual of theology. Its purpose is rather to place at the disposal of the reader interested in prayer and meditation the prayers of a great theological and spiritual teacher. What Rahner wrote in 1972 for the new edition of *Gebete der Einkehr* applies, with the necessary adjustments, to this entire book: "These prayers attempt by no means to belie their origins. . . . First of all, they express the concerns and anxieties of the scholar. But it is the sorrow and the joy shared by all Christians that impels me to write. Even the prayers of a priest, or one who wishes to become a priest, embrace all those who pray, for every Christian ought to know what quickens the human heart, the one to whom he entrusts his fate for all eternity."[6] The title of this anthology also demonstrates this in its own concise wording.

In his preliminary remarks on the present volume, Rahner made clear that such universal validity must not be equated with the immediacy required in the act of praying: "Obviously no one can simply offer the prayers printed on the page; no one can recite them before God just as they stand. They can hope to be no more than a stimulus to see this or that more clearly, to take to heart in one's own way, to say to God in one's own words that which might otherwise be overlooked, although (if one stops to think about it) it would deepen and enrich one's own prayer. And even if we seek to conceive, affirm, and formulate our own prayer, we can never know for certain whether the innermost core of our inward selves is praying too—there where, as St. Paul says, the Spirit of God intercedes for his saints with unutterable cries and where the Spirit of God prays that that which is unworthy be heard and discussed. But we simply must continue to pray, and to this end perhaps some such little help might prove beneficial. Private prayers formulated by individuals are entitled to be 'subjective.' They ought never to be reproached for that." Anyone wishing to pursue Karl Rahner's theoretical writings on prayer beyond this point is referred to the sermons he delivered in Munich in 1946 published under the title *Von der Not und dem Segen des*

[6]See note 2 above.

*Gebetes (Happiness through Prayer)* and reprinted since in many impressions and editions.[7] Finally, there are the complementary texts in the two Rahner anthologies, *Rechenschaft des Glaubens*[8] and *The Practice of Faith.*[9]

## Note to the Third Impression

Karl Rahner was able to receive this book in its first impression on the occasion of his eightieth birthday. His unexpected death on March 30, 1984, has turned this birthday present into a farewell gift. This new impression has made it possible to include in *Prayers for a Lifetime* probably his last text, composed on his sickbed, the "Prayer for the Reunion of All Christians."

[7]Most recently as vol 647 in the Herderbücherei (Freiburg, 1980, 10th edition). The English translation, entitled *Happiness through Prayer*, appeared in 1958 (Westminster, MD: Newman Press).

[8]See note 1 above; here pp. 348-62.

[9]Karl Rahner, *The Practice of Faith*, edited by Karl Lehmann and Albert Raffelt (New York: Crossroad, 1983) 84-101.

# SOURCES

*Encounters with Silence.* Translated by James M. Demske, S.J. Westminster, Md., The Newman Press, 1960. © 1960 by The Newman Press. Originally published as *Worte ins Schweigen* (1938). Reprinted along with *Gebete der Einkehr* under the title *Worte ins Schweigen, Gebete der Einkehr.* Freiburg: Verlag Herder, 1973.

*Everyday Faith.* Translated by W. J. O'Hara. New York: Herder and Herder, 1968. © 1967 by Herder KG. Originally published as *Glaube, der die Erde liebt.* Freiburg: Verlag Herder, 1966.

*Faith Today.* Translated by Ray and Rosaleen Ockenden. Sheed & Ward: London and Melbourne, 1967. Originally published as *Im heute glauben.* Einsiedeln: Benziger Verlag, 1965.

*Hilfe zum Glauben,* with Adolf Exeler and Joh. Bapt. Metz. Zurich: Benziger Verlag, 1971.

*Ich glaube an Jesus Christus.* Einsiedeln: Benziger Verlag, 1968.

*Mary, Mother of the Lord.* Translated by W. J. O'Hara. New York: Herder and Herder, 1963. © 1963 by Herder KG. Originally published as *Maria, Mutter des Herrn.* Freiburg: Herder, 1965[5].

*Meditations on Hope and Love.* Translated by V. Green. New York: The Seabury Press, 1977. © 1976 by Search Press Limited. Originally published as *Was sollen wir jetzt tun?* and *Gott ist Mensch geworden.* Freiburg: Verlag Herder, 1974, 1975. (The selections here are solely from *Was sollen wir jetzt tun?*)

*Prayers for Meditation,* with Hugo Rahner. Translated by Rosaleen Brennan. New York: Herder and Herder, 1962. © 1962 by Herder KG. Originally published as *Gebete der Einkehr* (1958). Reprinted along with *Worte ins Schweigen* under the title *Worte ins Schweigen, Gebete der Einkehr.* Freiburg: Verlag Herder, 1973.

*Servants of the Lord.* Translated by Richard Strachan. New York: Herder and Herder, 1968. Originally published as *Knecht Christi.* Freiburg: Verlag Herder, 1967.

*Theological Investigations VII: Further Theology of the Spiritual Life,* Vol. 1. Translated by David Bourke. New York: Herder and Herder, 1971. © 1971 by Darton, Longman & Todd Ltd. Originally published as the first part of *Schriften zur Theologie VII.* Einsiedeln: Benziger Verlag, 1966.

*Theological Investigations VIII: Further Theology of the Spiritual Life,* Vol. 2. Translated by David Bourke. New York: Herder and Herder, 1971. © 1971 by Darton, Longman & Todd Ltd. Originally published as the second part of *Schriften zur Theologie VII.* Einsiedeln: Benziger Verlag, 1966.

*Watch and Pray with Me.* Translated by William V. Dych, S.J. New York: Herder and Herder, 1966. Originally published as *Heilige Stunde und Passionsandacht* (1949). Freiburg: Verlag Herder, 1965[4].

God of My Lord Jesus Christ
from *Encounters with Silence*, pp. 11-17

In Praise of Creation
previously unpublished, translated by Elliot Junger

Christ All in All
from *Prayers for Meditation*, pp. 58-59

Prayer at Christmas
from *Theological Investigations VII*, p. 126

Reflection on the Passion
from *Watch and Pray with Me*, pp. 37-38

The Seven Last Words
from *Watch and Pray with Me*, pp. 39-63

The Presence of Jesus and His Life
from *Watch and Pray with Me*, pp. 9-16

The Presence of Jesus' Agony in the Garden
from *Watch and Pray with Me*, pp. 17-24

The Presence of the Agony of the Garden in Us
from *Watch and Pray with Me*, pp. 25-33

The Ascension and Presence of the Lord
from *Theological Investigations VII*, p. 180

The Imitation of Christ
from *Prayers for Meditation*, pp. 34-38

Following Christ Through Love of Neighor
from *Ich glaube an Jesus Christus*, p. 66, translated by Renate Craine

God's Word as Personal Promise
from *Ich glaube an Jesus Christus*, pp. 66-67, translated by
Renate Craine

Meeting Jesus
from *Ich glaube an Jesus Christus*, pp. 67-68, translated by
Renate Craine

The Holy Spirit
from *Prayers for Meditation*, pp. 44-48

Freed by God
from *Hilfe zum Glauben*, p. 56, translated by Renate Craine

God of My Daily Routine
from *Encounters with Silence*, pp. 45-52

The Life of Grace
from *Prayers for Meditation*, pp. 39-43

Prayer for Hope
from *Everyday Faith*, pp. 207-11

God of My Vocation
from *Encounters with Silence*, pp. 69-77

God of My Brothers
from *Encounters with Silence*, pp. 61-68

Prayer for the Church
previously unpublished, translated by Elliot Junger

Prayer on the Eve of Ordination
from *Servants of the Lord*, pp. 205-11

Prayer for the Right Spirit of Christ's Priesthood
from *Servants of the Lord*, pp. 213-16

The Sacrament of the Altar
from *Prayers for Meditation*, pp. 49-53

The Eucharist and Our Daily Lives
from *Theological Investigations VII*, p. 162

Prayer of a Lay Person
previously unpublished, translated by Elliot Junger

Prayer for Justice and Brotherhood
previously unpublished, translated by Elliot Junger

Prayer for Peace
previously unpublished, translated by Elliot Junger

Prayer for Creative Thinkers
from *Theological Investigations VIII*, pp. 130-32

Mary
from *Mary, Mother of the Lord*, pp. 104-107

Prayer to Saint Thomas Aquinas
previously unpublished, translated by Elliot Junger

God of the Living
from *Encounters with Silence*, pp. 53-59

God Who Is to Come
from *Encounters with Silence*, pp. 79-87

Between Grace and Judgment
from *Prayers for Meditation*, pp. 30-33

The Resurrection of the Dead
previously unpublished, translated by Elliot Junger

A Blessing on Our Ending
  from *Prayers for Meditation*, pp. 68–71

Prayer for the Reunion of All Christians
  previously unpublished, translated by Renate Craine

Closing
  from *Faith Today*, p. 48

Editor's Afterword
  by Albert Raffelt, translated by Elliot Junger